FINDING YOUR SELF

Liberation through
Advaita Vedanta

— Mithun Baliga —

ISBN: 978-1-7359791-0-6 (paperback)
ISBN: 978-1-7359791-1-3 (ebook)

This book is dedicated to my parents,
Dr. C.K Revathi Baliga & Dr. Dilip K Baliga,
who were my first *gurus*.

TABLE OF CONTENTS

Preface

The last few decades have seen a growing momentum in the search for something beyond the material. This renewed seeking has broken down conventional boundaries, as we reach across religions and nationalities to find answers. It has led to an unprecedented revival of ancient spiritual philosophies and texts. And in them, we find that the questions and doubts that plague us today, had also plagued our forefathers. These texts reveal to us ideas and concepts that are as relevant today as they were many centuries ago.

During my own seeking, I started exploring the concept of *Vedanta*, specifically *Advaita Vedanta*, and came across the text *Tattvabodha*. And not being fluent in *Sanskrit*, the ancient language of India, I sought out an English translation. Here, I was fortunate to read the English version by *Swami Dayanada Saraswati*. To say that this book mesmerized me, would not do it justice. It awakened something in me, something I thought was missing yet something I felt was inside me the whole time. I read it, read around it, dug up everything I could find in books and on the internet. I started learning the rudiments of *Sanskrit*. I began jotting down points as I wrestled to clarify the concepts in my head. Somehow, the book *Tattvabodha* and all related information from other sources came together and started to make sense for me in those notes. What started as a personal collection of notes has grown into the book you hold in your hand.

Tattvabodha is only one of the many books on *Advaita Vedanta*. But I found it to be a comprehensive, well encapsulated discourse, covering all the fundamental tenets of *Advaita* teaching and an excellent steppingstone to further studies. Therefore, I have used *Tattvabodha* as the guide in whose footsteps we shall follow in our quest to learn *Advaita*. I have tried my best to stay true to *Tattvabodha* as interpreted by the great *Swami Dayananda Saraswati*.

When pursuing *Vedic* studies, it is impossible to avoid the *Sanskrit* language entirely. Instead of trying to step around this issue, I have tried to embrace it in a small way without overwhelming the reader. Nothing should distract from the main task of grasping the concepts, so I pray that there is enough *Sanskrit* to flavor our study but not so much that it weighs us down.

I am merely a student of *Advaita Vedanta* and not an expert by any stretch of the imagination. I have stayed away from coloring the subject with my personal slant. But I have consolidated and arranged the knowledge in a way that I felt would make things easier to understand. In some instances, I have used the traditional examples quoted by great teachers like *Swami Dayananda Saraswati*, almost verbatim. In other places, I have tried to give contemporary examples and references to help relate to our present day. This book should serve as an introductory guide for a newcomer to the subject, as well as a refresher for those already familiar with *Vedanta*.

I would like to apologize for using the masculine pronoun by default. This is purely for the sake of convenience and not meant to exclude any gender from this study.

I humbly state that any errors or mistakes in this work are entirely my own for which I seek the reader's forgiveness.

I present this work in the fervent hope that it may open an enduring vista into spirituality for you.

Part I

–1–

INTRODUCTION

Almost everyone has heard of *Vedanta*. Many of us may even have a general understanding of what it is, or at least what we think it is. From my experience as a student I would like to share with you an outline of *Vedanta*. Our journey will be based on the framework provided by an ancient book called *Tattvabodha*. The word *tattva* means the truth, or 'the nature of' and *bodha* means knowledge. So, *Tattvabodha* means knowledge of the truth. We shall follow in the footsteps of *Tattvabodha* as we attempt to understand about our Self and seek the path to Liberation. *Tattvabodha* is a work written in prose form, that has been attributed to the famous 8th century philosopher and saint *Shankaracharya*. He was by far the most illustrious of all the proponents of *Vedanta* and his name lives on to this present day. There is some controversy about the authorship since the name

Shankaracharya is often taken by many philosophers in the *Vedanta* tradition. But we shall choose not to get mired in this particular controversy and focus instead on the actual teaching.

Tattvabodha is considered to be an introduction to *Vedanta* philosophy, a beginner's manual if you will. It is a steppingstone to *Vedanta* before taking on more challenging works like the *Bhagavad Gita*, the *Upanishads,* and the *Brahma Sutras*. It is also an introduction to many *Sanskrit* words and terms that are unavoidable in the study of *Vedanta*. The language is rich, with layers of meaning and I shall endeavor to guide us through some of the oft-repeating words. Becoming familiar with the words will enrich our experience and understanding of the material. From that point of view, *Tattvabodha* can also be viewed as a primer to the terminology of *Vedanta*.

When read for the first time, *Tattvabodha* can seem very confusing and we wonder: if something this abstract is only the beginner's book how can we ever grasp the rest? It can feel reassuring and intimidating all at once. It seems to clarify yet confound at the same time. However, the fault lies neither with the book nor the translation and/or the commentary. It is the ignorance that is inherent in us, the student/reader. When we have come as far away as we have from the teachings, even the very basics as outlined in this beginner's manual seem beyond our grasp. But with a little patience and discipline, it can be understood and absorbed in the spirit it was written.

Think of the subject matter as any other complex analytical problem-solving exercise. One is not to embark on this journey with lethargy or mental sloth just because we are reading a "religious" text. This book and this subject demand the application of acumen and intellect; the same as for any scientific or mathematical work. However, it also demands an open mind and clear discrimination. It will challenge us, the student, to look at all that we know, from a new perspective. This will take some getting used to, at least in the beginning. The key is not to give up but to remain steadfast in the quest. The journey and the destination are surely worth it.

THE STATE OF AFFAIRS

If you are completely happy in yourself, in your work, in your relationships and with your world in general, then you probably do not need to read this book; at least not right now. This is because you are already in a state of happiness. But keep the book on your shelf anyway. The need may arise at some point in life. I say this because, (as we will see later) the happiness derived from things and people around us is not of a permanent nature. So, there is a high probability that at some point in the future, when your state of happiness is less than complete or when you feel a desire to seek something more, the teachings of *Vedanta* might come in handy.

Oftentimes when we are young and strong, enjoying good health, wealth, and good fortune, drunk on our own power, we feel books and lectures on philosophy, spirituality, *Vedanta* etc. to be superfluous and a waste of precious time. We would rather be "out there", changing the world, making a difference, serving one's fellow men.

Only people who do not wish to actually "do" anything, indulge their time in studying these books and discussing such matters. Some may even deign to call them 'time wasters', who either have nothing to do or who use this as an excuse to do nothing.

Many of us will recognize ourselves as the speaker of the above lines.

But Youth fades. Life happens. To some of us it happens suddenly, without any warning. To some of us it happens in a gradual, barely perceptible slide. Health is lost, wealth and power too sometimes. Loved ones fall ill and or pass away. Relationships crumble, even the ones that we were sure about. Children grow up and acquire minds of their own and suddenly we feel neither young nor powerful. We feel like we have been woken up from a pleasant dream and pushed into a nightmare due to no fault of ours. We have done the right things; been faithful and hardworking, prayed whenever we could, have given to charity and volunteered for good causes whenever we could and yet we find ourselves unfairly dealt with.

This bewilderment can become many things, depending upon how we handle it. Practical people just take it to be the way of the world, roll up their sleeves and vow to try harder. Others sink from bewilderment into despair and depression of varying degrees. The ones that try harder, succeed to some extent before "life happens" again and the cycle is repeated. After a while, at the very least, exhaustion sets in and the gradual slide into unhappiness begins. There is much lashing about when a person is sinking. Friends and family who try to help are struck and hurt by the flailing limbs. They are given the impossible choice of staying and getting hurt or giving up and leaving. Many take the latter choice and leave, at least mentally and emotionally if not physically. Some even join the sinker.

Suddenly, within a short span of months to years, the young, powerful, perfect person is shaken to his core and is turned into an old, bitter, helpless victim, one whom the world has conspired to destroy.

Maybe things are not quite as bad yet. Even so it is still useful to understand the teachings of *Vedanta*.

Or maybe you are a person who has had everything in life all along and continues to do so. But somehow you have felt that there was something missing in life, something elusive, something you know you should have but are not sure what it is. The gradual nagging one day becomes a question that has to be answered. Again, *Vedanta* might come to your aid. But enough about the state of affairs. Let us look at the fundamental question.

The fundamental question

Vedanta is often referred to as a philosophy. This can give the misleading notion that it is a theoretical concept without much practical use. Nothing can be further from the truth. It is something to be understood and incorporated into everyday life. If it is not to be used, what use is a field of study? So, pay no mind to those who tell you that it has no practical application. *Vedanta* goes to the heart of the problem with the accuracy and single mindedness of an arrow.

The fundamental cause of our problem is one of identity.

"*Who am I?*" is the question that must be answered.

In a nutshell, having a mistaken idea of who we are is the primary cause of all unhappiness. Our mistaken ideas are not limited to our own sense of identity, they extend to how we see the world and reality itself. But that is only to be expected. If we cannot identify our own selves correctly how can we understand something as all-encompassing as reality? In other words, we are steeped in ignorance. We believe that the world actually works how we think it does. We are very knowledgeable about "how the world works", it is our playing field after all. This is where we live and work and succeed-until we don't. We only ever begin to question its workings when we fail to control it, when our "calculations" go wrong.

I have done the planning, I have put in the work, I have even factored in a Plan B, yet things have gone wrong!

This is usually when a slight doubt starts creeping in.

Maybe I don't understand the world completely after all. Maybe there is more to it than meets the eye. Maybe I have misread the playing field.

Usually, we will set these doubts aside and try again, with better, more accurate "calculations", only to be met with failure again.

This is the right time. This doubt about our understanding of the world is essential to undertake this journey.

Ask yourself this question. "*Who am I?*"

When someone asks us this, we reply with our name, title, job, or social designation depending on the context.

What is the answer when we ask this question of ourselves when we are alone? At home, standing in front of the mirror all by ourselves?

Tattvabodha answers this and other questions arising from this. The word *Tattvabodha* means knowledge of truth. We shall look into more detail about truth and what exact truth we are alluding to here. To start with we can take it to be knowledge of the truth about reality and ourselves. Knowing ourselves is the key and we can know ourselves only through intense study of the Self, which we call Self-Inquiry or Self-Knowledge. If we know ourselves, knowing the world is not very difficult. In fact, knowing oneself is the same as knowing everything.

– 2 –

THE SIX PHILOSOPHIES

B efore we enter into *Tattvabodha* proper, it is wise that we get a general idea of the various philosophies of life that existed in ancient India. These are complex matters and detailed descriptions are beyond the scope of our current discussion. So, I shall try to present a bird's eye view.

Ancient Indians were well known for their advanced knowledge of science and mathematics. They were also keen students of the human condition and the world around them. Study of life, sorrow and joy and the ultimate goal of human existence were topics of primary concern. The go-to, dependable source of all knowledge was the *Vedas*. The *Vedas* are scriptural works handed down generations. Their source is said to be divine, and not attributable to a human author/authors. The *Vedas* are believed to have been revealed to the ancient seers (called *rishis*) during their meditations. These were memorized and handed down from father to son or teacher to student and have thus been preserved. It is worthwhile to remember that we are talking about times when written language was yet to come into existence. So, these extensive tomes were committed to memory and passed on through oral tradition.

Now what do these *Vedas* contain? There are 4 *Vedas*: *Rigveda, Yajurveda, Samaveda* and *Atharvaveda.* They are each in turn divided into many portions or sections. For our purposes, we need to know that the first few sections each *Veda* give the rules and regulations for the right way of life. They explain in detail what is right and what is wrong (*dharma* and *adharma*). It does not so much tell us what to do, as tell us the consequences of path A, path B etc. Actions and their aftereffects are detailed along with many rituals and routines involved in daily life. The student under the tutelage of a teacher, would study these, understand them, and go forth to lead life with clear knowledge of the right and wrong way of life.

Now, there is a latter portion to the *Vedas*, which is referred to as *Vedanta* (*anta* mean the end, *Vedanta* means the end part of the *Vedas*). This portion is made up of texts called *Upanishads* and it deals with knowledge. Each of the four *Vedas* has its own set of *Upanishads*.

Again, the earlier sections of the *Vedas* are about actions and effects; the *Vedanta* portion, including the *Upanishads,* is about knowledge. It is in this latter part where the larger purpose of human life, the explanations as to an individual's identity, and the road to *Moksha* (or Liberation) are dealt with.

In short, there is a first action-based portion which guides us towards the achievement of material gains and a second, knowledge-based portion that guides us on attaining Liberation. It is this latter part, the *Vedanta*, which we are interested in.

As in modern times, the ancients were also in pursuit of the ultimate Truth about reality, a theory that unified everything. Again, as in the present, there were many philosophies or points of view to understand reality. Not everyone accepted the *Vedas* as the ultimate source of knowledge. Some lines of thought defied the *Vedas,* and those philosophies are called *Naasthik* philosophies. Those that acknowledged the *Vedas* as the supreme source of knowledge are called *Aasthik* philosophies. And not everyone who accepted the *Vedas* had the same point of view. We will take a look at the 6 *aasthik* philosophies. Please do not be overwhelmed by this, just read through them to get a general feel for the thought processes. In brief, they are:

1. *Nyaya* philosophy: This is a logic-based system. *Nyaya* means rules. It relies heavily on cause and effect and the sequence of cause and effect. For example, cause must precede the effect. It is closely allied to the next school of thought, the *Vaisheshika* philosophy.

2. *Vaisheshika* philosophy: A system that believes that the world is composed of atoms and their union and separation and the elements formed thereof are what determine the world and the forms and structures in it. *Nyaya* and *Vaisheshika* go together, in that the latter is about the structure and the former is about how to think about and understand that structure. These philosophers were critical thinkers, and they can be compared to modern day scientists.

3. *Sankhya* philosophy: This is an enumeration-based system. It is a dualistic view of the universe with two main entities, *Purusha* and *Prakriti*, being the cause of Creation. *Purusha* is the consciousness and *Prakriti* is the matter. The ancient Indian system of health and medicine, *Ayurveda* has its roots in this philosophy.

4. *Yoga*: *Yoga* means union; union of a seeker with his purpose. *Yoga* system is closely allied with

the *Sankhy*a philosophy's dualistic view and accepts the concept of *Purusha* and *Prakriti*. While *Sankhya* is more knowledge based, *Yoga* incorporated actions with knowledge. Using the knowledge in the *Vedas*, different ways of living life are expounded in order to attain union with the divine. The popular *asanas* or poses are only one of the 8 limbs of *Yoga*. The complete 8 limbs of *Yoga* called *Ashtanga Yoga* were described by *Patanjali* in his *Yoga Sutras*. *Patanjali* is believed to be an ancient yogi and mystic who codified the tenets of *yoga*. We shall take a look at the 8 limbs of his *Ashtanga Yoga* later (*pg. 64*).

5. *Mimansa* philosophy: This system believes in righteous living according to the principles of *Dharma* to attain Liberation. Based on the *Vedas*, it relies on rituals and directions on daily life as a path to Liberation.

6. *Vedanta*: This philosophy focusses solely on the attaining of right knowledge as the path to Liberation. Based on the *Vedas*, it involves studies of their latter portions, texts called *Upanishads*, the *Bhagavat Gita* and other scriptural works. The focus is on understanding human life and how to transcend from a limited entity to a limitless one.

All these were born in pursuit of the knowledge of reality. The ancient thinkers placed great importance not only on the acquisition of knowledge but also on the mode or means of attaining that knowledge. An independent means of acquiring knowledge is called a *pramana*. This is of some importance to us since we will encounter this term, *pramana*, in the coming sections. There are six different *pramanas*. They are:

1. Direct perception (*Pratyaksha*): This is knowing something by directly sensing it using our sense organs. For example, we see the flames and we know there is a fire.

2. Inference (*Anumana*): This is applying reason to the information gathered by the sense organs. For example, we see smoke from a distance and infer that there is a fire.

3. Comparison (*Upamana*): This is arriving at a conclusion by comparing and using analogy. For example, to a student who has never seen a zebra, we describe it as a four-legged animal with a tail, like a horse but it differs form a horse in that it has black and white stripes on its body. This should help the student correctly identify a zebra, when he comes across one, even though he has never seen one before.

4. Postulation (*Arthapathi*): This is postulating an explanation for facts that otherwise cannot be explained (by direct perception, inference etc.) using an already know fact. For example, Fact #1 he is a good student with high scores. Fact#2 He never studies in class. How is this possible? We postulate that he must be studying at home.

5. Negative proof (*Anupalabdi*): This type of *pramana* accepts knowing that something is not present as one way of gaining knowledge. For example, when we are searching for something, say our car keys, we look in all the usual places and by attaining negative proof in each place we search – not on the key hook, not in my hand bag, not fallen behind the sofa etc., we gain knowledge that the car keys are not inside our house.

6. Word (*Shabda*): This means of gaining knowledge accepts the word of unimpeachable sources, which in this case are the *Vedas*. There is an understanding that a person cannot gain all possible knowledge on his own in one lifetime, so he relies on the wisdom of learned men, teachers, and others. These could be in the form of oral or written tradition, but through words. The source has to be absolutely reliable and beyond doubt.

Now, all the six different philosophies do not accept all 6 *pramanas* as valid means of gaining knowledge and this is one of the important distinguishing features amongst the philosophies.

In summary, *Vedanta* is one of six philosophies to study reality. It also means the final essence or the end portion of the *Vedas*. *Vedanta's* main focus is on knowledge. It has withstood the test of time and over the centuries has endured as the corner stone of *Hindu* philosophy. In our pursuit of Self-Knowledge, we are going to turn to this source. It is important to realize that as with everything in Indian thought, *Vedanta* within itself has varied ways of understanding the same reality. The crux of the matter is always to understand the individual soul (the part, the small) with respect to the divine (the whole, the big): the relationship of one to the other, why they exist, if and how these two can be united.

Vedanta has 3 broad schools of thought: *dvaita, advaita* and *vishishtadvaita*, which differ in the way they describe this relationship.

Dvaita school is dualistic and says that the individual soul and the divine are two separate entities.

Advaita school is non dualistic and says that there is only one soul and that is the divine, the *Brahman*.

Vishishtadvaita school is qualified non dualism and

says that the individual and the divine are two separate entities, but the soul can attain union with the divine.

These are only very broad strokes as each one is an ocean in itself.

So now we have a better understanding of *Vedanta*; its definition and where it fits in the bigger picture. Attaining Liberation is the ultimate goal of spiritual practice. This Liberation is called *moksha* in *Sanskrit*, which implies freedom from all bondage and finally union with the divine. *Vedanta* guides one towards *moksha* through knowledge. *Vedanta* has been propounded and revived when revival was needed, by many great philosophers over the centuries.

One such philosopher was *Adi Shankaracharya* who shone the light of his unparalleled intellect on *Advaita Vedanta*. He was a renowned scholar who is believed to have lived around 7 – 8th century AD. He was known for his strong knowledge of the *Vedas* and he travelled the length and breadth of India teaching *Advaita Vedanta*. Using his formidable debating skills, he is said to have ascended the Throne of Wisdom (located near the contentious Line of Control in Kashmir) after vanquishing his peers from the other *aasthik* philosophies mentioned earlier. During his short lifespan of 33 years, he authored many discourses, treatises, and commentaries. He is considered to be the premier exponent of the *Advaita* school of thought. We should not make the mistake of saying that he "founded" this school of thought. He understood and explained the *Vedas* from a non-dualistic perspective and brought attention to the prescribed way to *moksha* as per the *Vedas*.

It is through *Advaita Vedanta* that we will attempt to seek Self-Knowledge in the rest of our discussion. And from here onwards when we say *Vedanta*, we are referring to the *Advaita Vedanta* school of thought.

— 3 —

THE FOUR
PURUSHARTHAS
(HUMAN PURSUITS)

As human beings, what do we do in our everyday lives? We wake up, eat what we can and get ready to go to work. A major portion of the day is spent at work and then we come home and take care of home life, take care of bodily needs, and go to bed. This sequence we repeat day after day. On weekends, we may devote some time to leisure; that long afternoon nap or we may watch a movie with friends and then again it is back to taking care of household chores or even work that has backed up. Some dedicated individuals might go to the gym or go on a trail hike or volunteer for their favorite charity. Every single activity in the above list satisfies some need in us.

All of us have wondered why we run around and do the things we do. How often have we observed a squirrel or a bird and felt that these animals lead a far more peaceful life than we do? Animals have two main priorities, feeding themselves in order to survive followed by the need to procreate. All competition and trials they face are related to those two needs. They do not climb a tree to lose weight. They do not groom themselves to improve their self-worth. What drives us as human beings? Our ancients have studied this in depth and have classified all human endeavors under 4 main categories. They are called the 4 human *purusharthas* or the 4 human pursuits.

As human beings we have 4 main goals. All our wishes, wants, and desires can be put under one of these four categories. They are usually listed as *Dharma, Artha, Kama* and *Moksha*. Although they are listed in this order, we shall look at them in a slightly different order. Later we will try to understand why they are listed the way they are.

1. *Artha*: *Artha* can be interpreted as wealth or security. All of us have the need to feel safe and secure. Everything we pursue that is directed towards achieving wealth which in turn gives us a sense of

security, come under *artha*. Food, clothing, shelter, earning money for now, saving money for the future, safeguarding our health, treating diseases etc. are all *artha*. Only after ensuring these can a person feel secure enough to seek the next *purushartha* or pursuit which is *Kama*.

2. *Kama*: This means anything that is considered a luxury. These are not necessary for security or basic survival, but they make life more comfortable, pleasant, and enjoyable. The arts, entertainment, the big house, the fancy car, the designer clothes etc. are considered *kama*. For people in some parts of the world, the circumstances are such that satisfying *artha* alone is difficult and they never make it to the *kama* stage. Once a person is secure in life and has luxuries he can enjoy, his mind then turns to the next *purushartha*, Dharma.

3. *Dharma*: This is the need to live a conscientious and righteous life. *Dharma* means doing the right thing irrespective of personal gain or loss. It can also be thought of as ethics and is considered to be invisible wealth. *Dharma* is a more refined and elevated pursuit than *artha* and *kama*. This is why *dharma* is listed before *artha* and *kama*. Then we move on to last one, *Moksha*.

4. *Moksha*: This can be translated as freedom or Liberation. Liberation from what? Liberation from the above 3 goals. Liberation does not mean that one should not pursue security, wealth, comforts, or righteousness. It means the presence or absence of these things do not affect the individual. Their presence does not overly please nor does their absence overly sadden. This is what it means to be free of something. It is freedom from bondage; bondage to the first 3 *purusharthas*. We will explore more about this pursuit in the next chapter.

There are some things that enslave us by their presence. They keep us in their hold and we often feel them to be a burden as well as a joy. E.g. money

There are others that enslave us by their absence. Without them our lives feel empty and worthless. E.g. relationships

We need to release ourselves from both these types of enslavement.

With the first 3 *purusharthas*, even after attaining them, our bondage to them continues. Just ask any rich man; he is always in the process of making more money, although he is already rich. Ask any beauty queen or model; she is always in the process of maintaining her beauty although she is already beautiful.

In contrast, after attaining the *purushartha* of *moksha*, we are freed from all pursuits. This is why *moksha* is the highest of the 4 human pursuits. It is considered to be our primary goal while *Dharma-Artha-Kama* are considered to be secondary goals.

It is important that we learn about these 4 goals right at the beginning. *Vedanta* is not about guilting us into not seeking wealth or comforts. It is not about renouncing everything and turning into an ascetic. We acknowledge from the start that since we are born as human beings, we have certain wants and needs which are unique to us. *Vedanta* seeks to educate us about these goals. Once we know about these *purusharthas*, then we can review our own goals.

What are the goals I have been pursuing? Are they more artha, or kama? Or dharma? Have I even thought of moksha?

Vedanta helps us do this and also shows us the order of importance of these pursuits so that we can dedicate our energies towards the more important pursuits.

Instead of denying these pursuits, we understand them as inherent human goals and try to attain them in a just way, while always moving towards the highest goal of *moksha*.

− 4 −

THE FOUR STAGES
OF LIFE

We are well aware that as we move through life, our wants, desires and goals keep changing. Again, just as our pursuits are classified into four categories, the stages of human life are also classified. This helps us put in perspective why we have the needs that we do at different times in life. It also serves as a roadmap, laying out the stages of life and what are the appropriate goals to pursue in each stage.

The 4 stages of life:

1. *Brahmacharya*: The student stage. Here the focus is on education. In the early times, on reaching the age of 5-7, we would be sent to live with a *guru* (teacher) in his home. The teacher would

have many such students in his care, who stay with him and learn the scriptures, the *Vedas*. In addition to scriptural teachings, the students' education included service to the *guru* and his household, maintaining their home and school. Learning servitude, humility, obedience, respect for elders and the society were woven in and emphasized. All skills required to become a productive member of society were also taught. When our education was complete (we would be a young adult by now), we would return to our home and pursue a profession or start a family. This entire first stage corresponds to our modern-day stage of schooling and higher education, be it going to college/university or into training. This was where the foundations about how to lead a righteous life were laid. The primary goal of this stage was to learn what is right and what is wrong or in better terms, learn about *dharma* and *adharma*. This knowledge was gained through the *guru*-guided study of the *Vedas* and other scriptures.

2. *Grihastha*: The family stage. Here we enter into the holy institution of marriage and start a family. In this stage, the *artha* and *kama purusharthas*

predominate. According to the laws of *dharma* or righteous living, we work, earn, spend, and save. We establish a family of our own and fulfill the responsibilities that arise therein. Again, the laws of *dharma* (as taught and imbibed in the *brahmacharya* stage), have to be heeded in how we go about doing all this. During this stage of life, which is the longest stage, we do not have time to reflect on the deeper aspects of life. The constant needs of everyday life and meeting those demands take precedence. In our roles as husband, wife, father, mother, employee, employer, we toil to do our best; earn money, buy a house, build a bank balance, plan for the children's education, our own retirement and so on. We do all this for ourselves and our children. In recent times, this stage of life has become more stressful and demanding on the average person than ever before, leading to early onset of stress related physical and emotional disorders.

3. *Vanaprastha*: The hermit stage. In this stage of life, we gradually withdraw from the *artha/kama* dominated *grihasta* life. In the ancient times, we would retire to the forest to follow a simple life, conducive to contemplation. We exit from a life

of material pursuit and prepare to enter a life of spiritual pursuit. We practice introversion, meaning we learn to be with oneself in solitude. We forgo seeking the constant presence of others. In current times, the incessant call of social media and news at our fingertips places an extra hurdle for us to clear. We have grown accustomed to the constant adulation of friends and strangers alike. Things have come to such a pass that having to even reduce some of this mindless interaction seems impossible. But that is what this stage is all about. We work towards getting comfortable with ourselves and not think of being alone as loneliness. We prepare the mind to be with itself because spiritual journey requires one to look more inwards than outwards. It serves to gradually train the mind to move away from looking without and be taught to look within.

4. *Sanyasa*: The renunciation stage. Here although we may not take the actual ritualistic renunciation, we live as if we have. The surrendering of worldly pursuits that started in the *vanaprastha* stage is complete. By now we have reached an age where there are no more demands on us to fulfill material wants. We can now choose to let go of

the trappings of the material world. Age and the wisdom that comes with it, make us realize that neither the body nor the mind is able to enjoy the comforts and luxuries that we chased after when we were younger. This also means letting go of our ego and ignorance, thereby readying us to gain Self-Knowledge.

Again, we see that the scriptures acknowledge that a person's life has various stages with the emphasis on different goals based on the stage of life. *Vedanta* does not ask that we give up everything from day one and live as a hermit. It provides a framework where we can morally attain our human goals while simultaneously preparing ourselves to work towards the higher goals of Self-Knowledge and Liberation.

– 5 –

THE FOUR QUALIFICATIONS

Now that we are aware of the need for Self-Knowledge, the question then arises, "How do I go about attaining it, while still living within the framework of the 4 goals and the 4 stages of life?"

The first step is to know and understand that there are certain qualifications required to embark on this journey. Just like we need to ensure that we have met the prerequisites to enroll in a course, we need to be aware of the requirements to study *Vedanta*. This is not to exclude people who do not possess the qualifications. It is to let the student know that these prerequisites are needed in order to understand and assimilate the material. If we find that we do not possess some of the qualities listed, all that we have to do is to spend some time attaining those first. This will greatly increase the chances of a successful study.

Many students get disillusioned with *Vedanta* because they find that even after studying and understanding it, they do not see much progress in their day to day life. Very often this indicates an incompletely prepared mind rather than a fault in *Vedanta* itself. *Vedanta* is a *pramana*. This means that it is an independent mode/instrument of knowledge. If it is correctly applied to a well-prepared mind, transfer of knowledge will take place.

Let us now look at the qualifications themselves.

1. *Viveka* – discrimination.

Right from the beginning, we have to clarify the use of the word discrimination here. It is not used in the now common negative meaning such as gender or racial discrimination. Discrimination means to be able to discern, to judge correctly. This can only be done when one has the right understanding. Now the question is: discriminate between what and what? What are the two things that are mixed up which we need to distinguish between?

White and black? Night and day?

No. These are obvious, and discrimination is easy. Here we have to remember that *Tattvabodha* says this discrimination is listed as a qualification. Without this we cannot be successful in the study of *Vedanta*. So, the discrimination we are referring to here must be between two things that are hard to distinguish from each other. The discrimination they mean is the ability to differentiate between permanent (*Nitya*) and impermanent (*Anitya*) things (*Nitya-Anitya Viveka*), between the eternal and the transient, in fact between real and apparent.

Let us take a look around us. Let us list some of the things we see.

House, tree, dog, friend, mother, cars, ocean, sky, sun…

Let us take a moment to consider which of these items are permanent and which are impermanent. It does not take much wisdom to realize that all living things like the tree, friend, dog, mother all have birth and death. They will all die one day, so they are impermanent. Inanimate things like houses and cars although do not have birth, have a limited life span. They will age and disintegrate as time passes. Items on the list like ocean, sky and sun may seem to be permanent when compared to the lifespan of a human but even they will come to an end one day. So, they are also impermanent.

By logic anything that has a beginning will have to have an end. Now we know that the entire universe exists within the construct of space and time. Everything contained within it, is subject to the effects of time, nothing can escape the relentless attack of time. Therefore, we can infer that in the universe nothing is permanent, everything will be subjected to birth and death. That is the very nature of things that belong in the space-time framework. So, there is no permanent object, no permanent person, no permanent situation, and no permanent relationship. This understanding is vital.

This is the nature of the world. This is the way it is for me, for you, and for everyone. It is impermanent, *anitya*. If we lean on anything in this world for permanent support, the inevitable result will be disappointment. Things in the realm of *anitya* cannot give us anything permanent.

Now what is permanent, or *nitya*? By our own inference it has to be something outside of the space-time framework. In *Vedanta*, we refer to this permanent entity as *Brahman*, the Self. We need to clarify that the word *Brahman* is different from *brahmin*. The latter is the word for those who belong to the priestly class. *Brahmins* were priests who officiated in temples and religious ceremonies. *Brahman* is also different from *Brahma*. The word *Brahma* refers to one of the gods of the *Hindu* trinity. He is the considered to be the Creator.

The other gods of the trinity are *Vishnu*, the Protector and *Shiva*, the Destroyer.

The *Upanishads* say that *Brahman* is permanent, pervasive, and subtler than the subtlest. They describe the nature of *Brahman* (or Self) as all pervasive like space; unborn, and eternal. And *Brahman* by very nature is *nitya* or permanent. This seems a bit difficult to understand now but will become clear as we proceed further and dive deeper.

2. *Vairagya* – dispassion.

Vairagya comes from the word *viraga*. *Raga* means to like or desire, the opposite of which is *dvesha* or dislike. *Viraga* means being without likes. In fact, it means to be without likes and dislikes. This is called dispassion. Dislike or aversion also comes under desire, except that it is a desire to avoid something. Where there is like, there will be dislike. Where there is desire towards one thing, there is also an implied aversion from another thing. So, it is impossible to choose one thing, without influencing the other. For example, when we say we like comfort, it is implied that we dislike discomfort.

In this context, like is to be taken to mean a *binding* attachment or desire. To have desires and dislikes is not wrong. It is quite normal and an essential aspect of survival. To have *binding* likes and dislikes is what is to be avoided. Binding desires are those which influence our actions. Binding desires are those that fill us with longing.

How do regular likes and dislikes turn into binding likes and dislikes? It happens when we place non- existent value or worth on certain things. We have falsely inflated the value of a particular object or person. This is called superimposition. Now since that object or person has become so valuable to us, we simply must have them or hang on to them at all cost. This error of superimposition happens in two ways.

One way is when we have mistaken one object for another more valuable one. An example of how this happens is when we walk into a store and want to purchase a fancy designer watch. We find one and buy it. What we do not realize is that it is a fake. We have mistaken the fake one for the real one. This type of superimposition occurs because of our incorrect assessment or incomplete knowledge of the object we were seeking.

The other way superimposition happens is when we have not mistaken the object for something else, but we err by adding value to it; value it does not truly possess. A typical example of this type of superimposition happens with money. Money is printed paper, which is used as currency, the primary use of which is to buy things. That is its true value. But what happens is that money or rather its buying power takes the place of security and happiness.

"If I have plenty of money, I will be happy and secure. Since I don't have enough money, I am insecure and unhappy."

Money gives us the power to buy what we want, yes. But how did we come to conclude that we can take our money to a store and "buy" happiness or security?

The logical explanation is that we have made an error of superimposition; we have accorded non- existent value to money by equating it to happiness and security.

Viraga means not committing either of these two mistakes but instead seeing things as there are. If viewed with complete objectivity, binding desires (or aversions) cannot arise. This is true *viraga*.

For example, the wife wants to go out for dinner, the husband wants to stay in.

She says, *"OK, then let's stay in."* And they end up staying in.

Although this was not the wife's original wish, she is fine with it even if she does not get her way. This is an example of having a desire, but it is not a binding desire.

In another scenario, she insists that they go out

because the thought of not going to that restaurant or the thought of her not prevailing, is too distressing for her and she engages in an argument. At the end of this the husband agrees to go out. This is an example of a desire that is binding. Because the desire influences her actions, makes her take steps to satisfy that desire, it is called a binding desire.

This is a very inane example, but it is just to shine light upon the meaning of binding desire and to help us look at our own actions (both big and small) from this point of view. I am sure we can come up with more serious and life altering examples.

To be free from this type of action-altering likes and dislikes is what is called dispassion. This is not to be mistaken for disinterest. *Vedanta* does not tell us to be disinterested in the world around us. What it goads us to do is to view our desires and aversions objectively and not let them influence our actions. In order to do this, we need that first qualification: discrimination. By using the power of discrimination (*viveka*), it becomes evident that fulfilling this one desire will not be a permanent solution or a permanent source of happiness. Then it automatically follows that we do not have to throw a tantrum or drastically alter our own actions or that of others to attain that desire. This is dispassion; dispassion born out of *viveka*. Sometimes dispassion is misinterpreted by some to be suppression of desires and/or hatred or disgust at worldly things. Again, this is not what we are seeking. What we are in search of is a balanced, objective mind.

Let us delve some more into why we seek *viraga*. What happens when we have strong, binding likes and dislikes?

When we nurse strong likes and dislikes, they influence our thoughts and actions. Our talents and skills are recruited to help us attain the object we like or avoid the things we dislike. Even if we succeed in attaining or avoiding things as per our desire, due to the very nature of the objects in this world, we are soon in need of doing this same exercise again. And so, the cycle of attaining and avoiding continues.

Therefore, the first qualification, discrimination, is put into use in the practice of the second, *viraga*. Once the discriminatory power of the mind (to know what is temporary and what is permanent) is activated, it follows that we will be dispassionate towards likes and dislikes, since *viveka* tells us that both are impermanent.

Another invariable effect of nurturing likes, and dislikes is that they distort our perception of the world. This subjective distortion will always stand in the way of someone who is seeking to explore the true nature of reality. So, by cultivating dispassion, we can see the world as it is, instead of viewing it through the tinted glass of our own perceptions (which are shaped by our likes and dislikes). By practicing *vairagya* or *viraga*, we will gain a stable and objective mind which is key to Self-Inquiry. The words to note here are "by practicing". We have to actually employ *viraga* in our everyday activities. Thankfully, life gives us plenty of opportunities to do so each day. Gaining mastery in *viraga* in mundane activities is a necessary first step before we can hope to exercise it successfully in more serious situations. Like everything else, *viveka* and *viraga* get better and easier with practice.

3. *Mumukshutvam* – desire for freedom

A burning, undeniable desire for freedom or *moksha* is called *mumukshutvam*. It is the desire for freedom from the problems caused by depending on the world. As human beings, all of us make this error. We rely on the world around us to fulfill our needs and wants. This dependence, which often goes unfulfilled, is what leads to the many problems that plague us. When a person enjoys a happy relationship or good financial position, he is worried that he will lose them and has to constantly work towards keeping these intact. The things that he depends on for his peace of mind and happiness sometimes come his way as per plan and all is well. At other times, irrespective of how much he tries, he is unable to hold on to them. These alternating successes and failures lead to feelings of insecurity, fear, frustration, and anger. The source of such problems is again, depending on the undependable, depending on impermanent things.

Man being the remarkable creature that he is, will do his best to overcome the "odds" and will try to attain his heart's desire. If he has decided that a particular relationship or a certain job is what it takes to keep him happy and secure, he will throw himself into working for it. When he realizes that even after all his hard work, that job or relationship is not guaranteed, he is saddened and hurt, paving the way for future mental and emotional issues.

It is not the fault of the world that I am unable to gain any semblance of permanent peace of mind or happiness from it. The world was never designed to give me or anyone else this permanent happiness and permanent peace. If I assumed that I could make the world give me that which I desire and I am now disappointed, it is my own fault.

This never-ending suffering, we all experience because of our wrong expectation and dependence on the world is called *Samsara*.

The firm desire to be free from this *samsara* is *mumukshutvam*. And a person seeking it is called *mumukshu*.

Why is this desire listed as a qualification?

A person can have many desires. And in this constantly moving, churning world, only the most important desires take priority. That is why *Tattvabodha* urges that attaining *moksha* should be our first desire, so that all the activities we do will be directed towards fulfilling this goal. This should be our primary desire and all our other desires should serve to fulfill the primary desire.

At this juncture, you may ask, "Isn't desiring *moksha* a form of like/dislike, *dvesha/raga* tangle, again leading us into the web of desire?"

Yes, but the desire for *moksha* leads us down the path of discovery of the Self, of knowing oneself. When we understand the Self, our true nature, we will be free. And our true nature is that we are already free. So, although it looks like we are again running towards a goal (that of *moksha*), we are in fact running back into ourselves to discover that we are already free.

Desire for *moksha* is the only desire that keeps us focused on the Self, whereas every other desire makes us focus on the world outside. Therefore, *mumukshutvam* amounts to a desire for the Self that leads to the knowledge of the Self, which culminates in freedom from all desire.

In fact, this is the only desire that can be fulfilled. If we think about things for a while, we realize that we are unable to fulfill any desire absolutely, although we may entertain various desires. Because behind all desires is really the desire for freedom and we are willing to do anything to gain that freedom. In fact, the truth is that nothing we *do*, can give us that freedom. "Doing" in and of itself creates results that we can satisfy ourselves with only temporarily. After a while, the feeling of unfulfilled desire returns, and the cycle continues. What if there were to be a desire, which when fulfilled can give us lasting satisfaction?

Yes, there is. That desire is *mumukshutvam*. In reality, there is no desire other than *mumukshutvam* that can ever be fulfilled. Why is this?

The desire for freedom can be fulfilled because freedom is our very nature. Even the desire for freedom would be an obstacle to the goal if freedom were something to be achieved by performing actions.

Since the Self is already free, this desire for freedom can be fulfilled. Knowledge of the Self (and its already free nature) is what brings about this freedom.

Mumukshutvam, therefore, is a desire for attaining that which is already attained.

4. *Shatka Sampattihi* – Six-fold discipline

The fourth qualification is discipline. *Shatka* means six. There are 6 aspects in which we have to attain discipline. I have listed them below. These are just short descriptions, without going into great detail, just enough to get an understanding.

- *Shama*: *Shama* means tranquility of the mind or mastery over the mind. We are all well aware how easily the mind is distracted. Even in simple pursuits, the mind strays from the task at hand and only with effort can we bring the mind back on track. Our mind is a tool, and we need to pay attention to its workings. It is not to be taken for granted neither is it to be viewed as the creator of our problems.

In our case, we need a mind that can stay tranquil or quiet for prolonged periods in order to listen, absorb and practice the teachings and the path of Self-Knowledge.

- *Dama*: *Dama* means control over the sense organs. Again, the pursuit we are engaged in requires us to focus on teachings for long periods of time. We know that if not our mind then our sense organs distract us. We have sat down to contemplate or meditate on the teachings; and our ears hear sounds from the street and distract us. Our skin itches and we want to change our position. The eyes feel uneasy and we want to open them. Our mouth suddenly wants to taste the dessert that we know we have put aside in the fridge, and so on, and all this is just during one meditation session!

True *dama* is to have control over our sense organs at all times. A good example is the tongue, which is used for both speech and taste. The lack of control over the desire for taste leads to a wide variety of food and weight related disorders. Of all our sense organs, eyes play a particularly important role, because the majority of our sensory input comes from our eyes. This is why we are asked to close our eyes during meditation. Much of the distraction can be controlled by closing the eyes.

Vedanta does not say that we should suppress our sense organs. It only says that when we want to focus on something, we should be able to do so without being distracted by our sense organs. We should be the master of our mind and sense organs, and not the other way around. We should not be enslaved by our senses. Only when they distract us from doing what we have set out to do, should the issue of control and restraint come in.

- *Uparama*: *Uparama* means introspection or focusing the mind on what we want it to focus on, in our case the study of *Vedanta*. The mind and sense organs that have been mastered by *shama* and *dama* are now engaged in *uparama*. *Shama* and *dama* need a lot of effort to achieve but once they are attained, *uparama* is relatively easy.

When the mind is interested in a particular goal, it automatically finds the time and energy needed to pursue it. Just look at any child who wants to play his favorite video game. He may not have to time to work on his summer project, but there is always time to play his video game.

When the mind senses something superior, its interests in inferior things fall away automatically. So, cultivating a superior interest makes the senses and the mind be more abiding. Worldly things are attractive to the senses and the mind, only in the absence of a superior pursuit.

Thus, if we want to free our minds from the fascination of worldly objects, it is necessary for the mind to be shown something better. As a first step, we discipline our minds and sense organs; later we expose our minds to something more subtle, more beautiful; something that lies within.

The idea is that beauty and happiness are both present within the Self. As we understand the beauty that the scriptures reveal to us as being inherently present, the need of the mind for gross beauty drops off slowly and the mind becomes abiding.

A time will come when the mind and sense organs will become abiding effortlessly; they will then have discovered an inner poise, silence, or joy. This state is called *uparama*.

- *Titiksha*: *Titiksha* means forbearance. It is the endurance that is required to go through the various ups and downs of life. It is easy to see how a person can go astray when in the "down" part of life's swing, but it is equally easy for a person to lose their way when things are in the "up" part of life. The inner strength that is required to go through both the positive and negative experiences in life is *titiksha*. It is a close relative of the first qualification, *viveka*. *Titiksha* is the ability to retain our equanimity irrespective of the situation. This is not merely maintaining an outward calm while seething and smoking on the inside. It is internal endurance.

- *Shraddha*: *Shraddha* means trust or faith. For most of us, the very word, faith, brings with it a certain skepticism. This is because we take it to mean blind faith. That is not the kind of faith or trust we mean here. *Shraddha* refers to a non-critical open mindedness where we give the benefit of doubt to the scripture or teacher, until we understand the material for ourselves.

In the beginning of any study, we may come across things we do not understand. When this happens in the study of *Vedanta*, we keep an open mind and say, *"I do not get this. But let me explore further and try to understand it and see."*

This is *Shraddha*. This kind of humility is a safeguard against intellectual arrogance.

- *Samadanam*: *Samadanam* means concentration. We are now in possession of a mind over which we have gained control, we have also gained control over the senses, attained forbearance, and cultivated *shraddha*. A mind thus prepared is now ready. It is ready to concentrate on the subject of *Vedanta*.

All the above comprise the six-fold discipline required to embark on Self-Inquiry according to *Tattvabodha*. Again, we should not be disheartened by the long list of things to do before we can start our journey into *Vedanta*. These things that we have to achieve are not separate from our study but are rather an integral part of the study.

– 6 –

KARMA YOGA

Now, all of us are not going to be in possession of the 4-fold qualifications at the start of our journey. But that does not matter. The desire to go on the journey is foremost. The above paragraphs only list and define the requirements but do not give us the actual way by which to attain them. When we realize that we are lacking in qualifications, as most of us will be, we want to know how to qualify ourselves. This is what we will focus on the next few sections.

The idea is for the student (who is called a *sadhaka*) to attain the goal (the *sadhyam*). Once he has attained the goal, he is called a *siddha*. The disciplined way to train oneself is through a series of *yogas*. The word *yoga* means to unite. In the current context, it means to unite *sadhaka* with his *sadhyam*. The *yoga* referred to here is not the physical *asanas* (poses) based *yoga*. It refers to a disciplined way of life, with recommendations about how to view life, the world around us, our own actions in the world etc. By practicing the prescribed *yogas* at the recommended stages of the journey, we can attain the qualifications and then move on to eventually attain *moksha*. Let us list the three types of *yoga* involved. All three must be applied at different stages in order to attain the different qualifications.

- *Karma yoga*
- *Upasana yoga*
- *Jnana yoga*

Karma yoga: Let us start with this first one. *Karma* can be translated as "right action" and *yoga* here can be translated as "right attitude". So, *karma yoga* is doing the right action with the right attitude. Let us address "right attitude" first before we go to "right action".

So, what is the right attitude to have? The right attitude starts by having the correct understanding about how the universe works. We accept that, "Every action has an equal and opposite reaction" and "An object at rest or in motion will continue to stay in that state until acted upon by another force" (Newton's laws).

I bring this up here to point out that objects in

this known world are subject to different forces which change/alter the behavior of these objects accordingly. The final position of the object depends on the starting point of the object, attributes of the object itself as well as those of the forces acting on it.

Let us look at our actions from a similar perspective. Once we perform an action, it has left our hands, so to speak. Now we might have performed this action (which may be highly intelligent, well thought through etc.) with a certain end result in mind. But between us performing the action and the action reaching the target, it must traverse a "field" where the forces of the Universe are in play. Often, we forget about the existence of this field. So, every time we perform an action, it leaves our hands and is acted upon by forces in the field, which are in fact the laws of the Universe (which can be called *Isvara* or God, if you will). These laws act on everything in Creation and are also universal. After being acted upon by the laws of the Universe we see our actions hit/miss (in varying degrees) the target and come back to us in the form of the results of our actions or the "fruits". This explains why sometimes our actions, no matter how well thought out or planned or well intentioned, may go very wide off the mark, filling us with confusion, disappointment and even anger.

The *Bhagavad Gita* puts this beautifully, "You have

choice only over your actions. Do not at any time think you are the author of the results of the action; neither be attached to inaction."

Some of us may be familiar with the verse. But there is wisdom buried in many layers in these few words directed at addressing the right attitude towards any action. It tells us that there is an arc from action to result. There are parts of the arc over which we have control and parts over which we don't. Choosing what action to do is what we can control, the end result is always out of our hands. Now after hearing this, we can ask,

"So, if I cannot be guaranteed the result I want, why should I perform the action at all? I'd rather not do it."

Especially in this day and age where everything is result oriented, this is not a strange question to ask. Even a child wants to know what is in it for her before she agrees to do anything. The *Bhagavad Gita* anticipates this line of thought and advises that we should not take refuge in inaction either. Irrespective of the end result, action that is in accordance with *Dharma* has to be performed. This is the right attitude with which we should do any action. And this is the main pillar of *Karma yoga*.

Every action is called a *karma* and *karma* thus processed by the Universal laws is called *phalam* (result). We will study *karma* in great detail later (*pg. 232*).

Let us examine "right attitude" in light of this. Whenever we perform an action or *karma*, we are in fact sending it to the Universe or *Isvara* or God. Therefore, it is an offering to God. Likewise, when we receive a result or the *phalam*, for that action, it comes to us from the Universe/*Isvara*/God. The scriptures point out that the universal laws are tools in the hands of Universe/*Isvara*/God to maintain the harmony of creation and therefore when we say the laws are processing the *karmas*, it essentially means God is processing them through the tools of his own universal laws. Therefore, *karma* is going to God for processing and is coming from God in a processed form called *phalam*. What comes from God is considered to be *prasad* or blessing. In places of worship, at the conclusion of the prayer, a fruit, or a flower is given to the devotee by the priest or whoever is officiating the prayer. During prayers at home, the parent, usually the mother will distribute this *prasad* to the rest of the household. It will usually be a very simple thing like a piece of sugar candy, or some raisins or fruit. We are not allowed to ask for a specific item to be given to us. Whatever the mother gives is taken to be the right *prasad* for us. This *prasad* is thought of as a blessing from God and therefore sacred. It cannot be rejected or criticized and is received with a sense of fulfilment, be it in the place of worship or at home.

Once we re-tune our minds to see our actions and their results as offerings to and blessings from God, our outlook towards our actions changes. With this attitude our mind gains equanimity. Every action is done with joy and utmost respect as it is an offering to God/Universe and not merely a solution to a problem or plan to achieve something. Similarly, every result is accepted as a blessing. This is what is meant by "right attitude".

Now let us examine what is "right action". As mentioned earlier, every action is called a *karma*. According to our scriptures, there are 3 types of actions or *karmas*.

- *Sathvik karmas*: These are actions that are more "giving" than "taking". They are acts of selfless service that benefit the people and the world around us. They are actions that do not arise from our own likes and dislikes (think back to *viraga*). These are not skewed by our perceptions. These are considered to be the best types of actions. They advance us spiritually.
- *Rajasic karmas*: These are actions done for our own benefit, like seeking materialistic pleasures for ourselves. They may serve us to attain some of the first three *purusharthas* but are spiritually stagnating *karmas*.

- *Tamasic karmas*: These are actions that grab more from the world around us and even cause harm to those around us. Damaging the world or the environment in pursuit of our own desires, hurting people around us in anger are some examples of *tamasic* karmas. These are spiritually regressive actions. Sometimes we are forced to do some tamasic actions like kill bugs or maybe tell a white lie. But we can make up for these unavoidable *tamasic karmas* by doing more *sathvik karmas*.

So, the right action is to choose our actions to be of a *sathvik* nature.

What happens when we practice *karma yoga*?

When we choose *sathvik* actions and perform them with dispassionate objectivity, that is we do them with the right attitude, then neither the action nor its results create distress or bondage in the mind. If we take the time to reflect, it is never the action that causes us discomfort, it is always the anticipation of the results that brings about turmoil. It is this reaction of the mind to the results of action that creates the emotional and mental agony.

For example, a student is ready to take a standardized test that is crucial for getting into the college of his choice. His anxiety before the test needs no description. We have all been there.

If we think about it, *"Is it the actual writing down of answers in the test that is causing him the anxiety?"*

No. It is the final score that he is going to receive on the test that is causing him the panic and fear. By detaching the mind from the result and keeping it focused on the action, which is within our power to perform well, we overcome distress and fear.

So, by practicing *karma yoga*, as described above, we become free from feelings of distress and helplessness. In short, the mind stops reacting to the so- called unexpected results of actions.

A reacting mind can never be a learning mind. Learning can only take place in a calm, receiving mind; not one that is filled with helplessness, frustration, and despair. We are often told that experience is a great teacher. Although that is true, we can only learn from the experience of our actions if our mind is in a non-reacting state. Otherwise we may undergo lesson after lesson, experience after experience and not learn anything and only become more and more angry and bitter. Actions done through *karma yoga* result in a mind that has equanimity, thereby rendering it conducive to learning from "experience". This is the true gift of *karma yoga*.

— 7 —

UPASANA YOGA

Upasana Yoga: This practice can be summarized as conditioning of the personality. In broad terms the physical body, the sense organs and the mind contribute to our notion of personality. All these three have to be properly conditioned in order to embark on our journey towards *moksha*. One of the sense organs, speech (called *Vak*) is so important that, that we will look at it in its own right, making four separate areas of conditioning.

To understand our journey through life towards the goal of *moksha*, this analogy is often used. Visualize a chariot journeying towards its destination (*moksha*). For successful completion of the journey, the chariot has to be in good condition (the physical body), with a smart driver (good intellect), with reins held firmly (a disciplined mind) and horses under control (good control of the sensory organs). *Upasana yoga* is the method to attain such a vehicle for our journey.

Under *Upasana yoga* we have physical conditioning, verbal or speech conditioning, sense organ conditioning, and mind conditioning.

Physical conditioning is easy to understand. This refers to taking care of the physical body, not necessarily with luxuries but by not polluting or tampering with it. A nutritious, mindful diet and adequate exercise to keep the body healthy is important in this journey. Overindulgence, even in the name of health can often lead to its own problems. If the physical body is not appropriately cared for, the chariot will break down, and the journey will not be possible.

Next is verbal conditioning. This always starts by being mindful of our words. Both the quantity and quality of speech are equally important. On reflection, we can all agree that many problems arise simply by speaking too much. Thinking before speaking should become a habit and not the other way around. The words we use; are they meant to cause hurt or pain? The words we speak; are they the truth or filled with lies? Every time we open our mouth to speak, we should examine with care the intention, content, and mode of our words. Control over speech is particularly stressed since it is the most common tool we use to abuse or hurt others. And if bad or distressing things must be said and are unavoidable, we should endeavor to say them in the kindest way possible.

Conditioning of the other sense organs is the next step. In today's world this has to be emphasized in a way that was not needed a few decades ago. The constant presence of social media like Facebook, Twitter and Instagram in our lives flood us with all kinds of input to our sense organs. The eyes are made to see countless images, the ears hear speeches, songs, and words more than any generation of humans ever have and the typing fingers fly across the keys with dizzying speed. All of us are in a rush to stuff our minds with information and are compelled by the need to comment on things first, with the most force and to garner maximum number of followers. None of us ever stops for a minute to think if these bits of unconnected information are really important to our lives. Only an exceedingly small percentage of what we consume via these channels is actually worth our while. The rest just act as fodder for our brain and mind. Our mind is a marvelous instrument but that is what it is, an instrument. It can be used well, or it can be abused till it destroys itself.

Sensory conditioning means carefully choosing what we want to expose our senses to. Too much exposure to violence for example leads to a kind of conditioning whereby the person becomes numb to it and starts thinking that it is part of normal behavior. So, our very plastic mind is conditioned by what we choose to put in it. And we put things in our mind via the sense organs. They are the portals of entry into our mind.

With this knowledge, each of us must exercise our right to expose our senses only to what we think will be good for our mind, only to things that will help us in our journey. We do not simply eat whatever is put on our plate just because it is there in front of us. Similarly, we cannot feed our senses with whatever is thrust before them. We have to exercise our right to turn away from sensory inputs that will harm our mind. This turning away is a sign of strength not weakness.

Mental conditioning is the last step. The mind is a very subtle organ, not easily understood. That is why this is mentioned last. We can get to it only in steps; by gaining mastery over the body, the speech, and the senses, since all these are doorways to it. *Ashtanga yoga* of *Patanjali* is a form of *yoga* practice that details how to attain this control over the mind. *Ashta* means 8 and *anga* means limbs, so *Ashtanga yoga* is the 8 limbed yoga practice as described by its founder *Patanjali*. The complete 8 limbs of *Yoga* as described by *Patanjali* in his work, the *Yoga Sutras* are:

1. *Yamas*. These are the moral rules that must be followed by all. They are the "don'ts" These dictate our actions towards others. They are
    *   *Ahimsa*: nonviolence
    *   *Satya*: not lying, truthfulness
    *   *Astheya*: not stealing
    *   *Brahmacharya*: sexual restraint
    *   *Aparigraha*: non greed, non-possessiveness
2. *Niyamas*. These are the rules about our behavior towards ourselves. They are the "dos". They are
    *   *Sauchya*: cleanliness
    *   *Santosha*: being content
    *   *Tapas*: austerity, perseverance
    *   *Svadhyaya*: self-study, study of scriptures
    *   *Ishvarapranidhana*: contemplation of *Ishvara*/the Supreme/Brahman
3. *Asanas*. These are the well know poses of *yoga* practice. Actually, *Patanjali* defines *asana* as posture that can be held for prolonged periods without any discomfort. The word *asana*

means a comfortable posture conducive to meditation.

4. *Pranayama.* This is the control of breath. After attaining a good posture, regulation of breath is instituted by different techniques of inhalation, exhalation and breath holding.

5. *Pratyahara.* It is the withdrawal of the mind from sensory stimuli. This does not mean disconnecting ourselves completely from all sensory input. What it means is keeping the mind away from the influence of the sensory inputs.

6. *Dharana.* This means concentration, establishing a one-pointed focus on a topic. It could be chanting a *mantra* or thinking about a deity.

7. *Dhyana.* This is the logical next step. It means contemplation. It is uninterrupted stream of thought or flow of awareness about the object we concentrate on in *dharana*. It is the process of the mind.

8. *Samadhi.* After *dhyana*, comes *samadhi*. Here the meditator is so deep in meditation that he becomes one with object of meditation. The mind loses its identity and the meditator, the object of meditation and the meditation process merge in to one.

Figure 1. Patanjali's 8 Limbs of Yoga

As we can see, the 8 limbs are set up in such a way that they cover physical, sensory, speech and mind conditioning. Another thing to observe is the progression of the course of discipline from the physical level to the mental level, from external to internal. We discussed *Ashtanga yoga* because it covers all aspects of *Upasana yoga* in an orderly manner. They are not synonymous, and this is not an endorsement for *Ashtanga yoga* in any way. But *Patanjali's* wisdom about the importance of conditioning the body, senses and mind is so emphatic and profound that learning about *Ashtanga yoga* will benefit us all, irrespective of which type of *yoga* practice we follow.

One of the main tools used to condition the mind is meditation. Nowadays many kinds of *yoga* and meditation practices are available, making it hard to decide which one to choose. However, if it is to be successful, all forms of meditation should include the first three steps namely physical conditioning, speech, and sensory organ conditioning to some extent before or at least along with the actual meditation. We will not go into the different techniques of meditation or discuss the pros and cons of different techniques.

But what we will do is take this chance to clarify what meditation is and what it is not. Meditation is not *moksha*. Meditation is not enlightenment. Meditation is an experience, just like any other experience. It is a tool to aid in Self-Inquiry. It does this by conditioning the mind, by clarifying the mind, by stilling the mind. In this now clear mind, Self-Realization appears like the reflection of the moon in a still pond. But since it is an experience, it ends; leaving the meditator feeling disappointed that he or she cannot hold on to the Self-Realization that was briefly glimpsed. This is an oft encountered situation where long-standing meditators get stuck in the stage of meditation without attaining enlightenment or Self-Realization. The enlightenment they seek can only happen when they realize that one is not the meditator but the one who knows the meditator (this shall be explained at great length later).

Instead, meditation when done with the right preparation sets the stage for the next type of *yoga, Jnana yoga. Jnana* means knowledge. Knowledge unlike experience does not end. Even after the experience ends, knowledge remains. And this knowledge we are referring to is the knowledge of the Self. This is why meditation is not considered a *pramana*, meaning it is not an independent means to gain knowledge. The meditator often thinks that he/she has experienced the Self in deep meditation, when in fact the Self is always with us. So, we should be experiencing it at all times.

The way to look at it is to move from the experience that is granted to us (when the chaos of the mind is stilled) in meditation, to the knowledge of the Self which should be ever present in us. We are always experiencing the Self whether we are meditating or not, in *samadhi* or not, whether our *Kundalini* is awake or not, etc. We just don't know this. Gaining this knowledge is *Jnana yoga*. In the upcoming chapters, this is what we will be focusing on.

Let us quickly review the 4 qualifications that were

listed earlier. They are *viveka* (discrimination), *vairagya* (dispassion), *mumukshutvam* (burning desire for Liberation), and *shakta sampatihi* (six-fold discipline). So far, we have listed them and explained what they were. We also saw the different types of *yogas* we can perform to attain those qualifications. Now I would like to go a step further and match the qualification we are seeking, to the *yoga* best suited to attain that qualification.

The way to attain the first three, *viveka, vairaghya* and *mumukstvam* is by practicing *Karma Yoga*. The way to attain the fourth one, *shakta sampatihi,* the six-fold discipline, is through *Upasana Yoga*. These also help us in attaining the first three *purusharthas* we saw earlier- *Dharma-Artha-Kama*.

But to attain that last or the primary *purushartha, moksha*, we need *Jnana Yoga*.

Hopefully, this has put in perspective these different types of *yogas* and where they are to be used. They are not three different paths towards *moksha*. One cannot say, "I will follow *Karma Yoga"*, "I will follow *Upasana yoga"*, or "I will follow *Jnana yoga"*, to attain *moksha*. All three must be employed at different stages of the journey. Therefore, all the 3 types of *yoga* are important in the pursuit of Self-Knowledge.

– 8 –

ON HAPPINESS

B efore we move further, let us take a short detour into the subject of happiness. Whenever we ask someone, *"What do you want for yourself?"*, the answer most often will be *"happiness"*.

Now we need to look closer into this happiness which we all seek. According to us, in order to make us happy, happiness must possess a few qualities. It has to be lasting and permanent. We are not satisfied with happiness that disappears after a while. We do not want happiness that is bound by time or situation or place or person. We want happiness that is present at all times and in all situations, in all places irrespective of the persons present.

And yet, we seek to capture this happiness (which should be lasting and permanent) by attaining a particular person, situation, place, or time. Somehow in some part of our brain, we think that if we get the perfect partner, the right job, the perfect body, we will miraculously become happy. When viewed together, it is plain that we are going about it the wrong way and it is evident why we get disappointed time and again. We are in search of something permanent and we try to get it by going after impermanent things.

Actually, the list of requirements for the happiness we seek does not end there. We want to have this happiness without having to make much effort, we want happiness to be effortless. What a tall order! But wait we are still not done. There is one more quality we want: awareness. In deep sleep for example, we are completely happy, but we are not aware of it! The final criteria is that we want to be aware of this boundless, permanent, effortless, unconditional happiness. No wonder what we seek is so elusive!

Now let us think some more and get into the nuts and bolts of happiness.

Where does happiness lie? Does it lie in the object/action?

Let us assume that it is so. But the object/action that gives me great happiness causes unhappiness to someone else. In my spare time, I may love going to the rock-climbing center and climb the most difficult of courses, or I may love riding rollercoasters because these actions give me great happiness. But these same actions are a source of mind-numbing fear and panic to my best friend. So clearly the object/action does not "possess" happiness on its own. If that were so, a particular object possessing say 10 lbs of happiness, should deliver that 10 lbs of happiness to anybody who owns it, irrespective of the individual. We have to smile, since we know that is not true.

Is it in me, the person, the seeker?

We are tempted to say yes. Yes, happiness lies in the individual seeking it. Yet consider this. A person is given an object today and he feels very happy, but when he is given the same object say next week, for some reason he is not happy or is even unhappy with it. Does that mean happiness doesn't even lie with me, the person? We find that hard to believe.

If happiness is neither in the object nor in the seeker then where is it?

We have all been in situations where we have desired a particular object, situation, or person. We know well the thrill and drive with which we seek it out and work towards attaining it. And finally, when we do get it, we know that we feel happiness. (Now it is beside the point that that hard-won happiness may or may not last very long and then we want another object or person.)

Even though we may not be able to pinpoint where exactly happiness lies (in the action or in me, the person), the happiness we feel when we attain the object of our desire is very real indeed.

So how does this come about?

Let us analyze this further.

What happens when we attain the object of our desire?

We stop seeking.

Until we get what we desire, the mind is restless. When we attain what we want, the restlessness is resolved, and the mind is satisfied. We stop doing any action towards the attaining of the goal. We do not all chase the same objects or people or situations, because only certain objects and individuals please us. And that is based on our background, values our own personal likes and dislikes etc.

But, the happiness we feel when we finally acquire something, never comes from the objects or the people attained. The cessation of seeking is what causes happiness. When the seeking is removed, there is nothing left except the true us, the true Self. When we are finally still and not "doing things", not seeking (because we have just attained the object), in the stillness, we experience our true Self, which is always in a state of permanent happiness. The Self- because of which we are aware of our body, our emotions, our thoughts and all the objects in the world- is therefore the source of the happiness.

Happiness is manifest only in a satisfied mind, a mind that desires nothing, because the Self is the source of happiness. The unqualified joy that we feel when we see something beautiful or hear a child laugh is an expression of our own inner happiness.

According to our own requirements which we listed earlier, we want something that is permanent, lasting, effortless, and filled with awareness. This is almost exactly how the scriptures describe the Self, *Atma* or *Brahman*. (For now, these terms can be seen as synonyms, in the later chapters, we shall understand how and why *Atma* and *Brahman* can be used interchangeably.) Only the Self or *Brahman* can provide lasting happiness or lasting security. *Brahman* alone is unqualified with reference to time, place, or condition and, being the very Self, the attainment of *Brahman* is effortless. *Brahman* is also awareness itself.

So, our true nature, our true self, which is Self/*Atma* or *Brahman* is always in a state of happiness. Finding and identifying our true Self (not our present "I" that we take to be who we are) is the only way to get that happiness we described earlier (unqualified, permanent, effortless and with awareness).

We are all already in a state of permanent bliss. But we do not know it because, as mentioned in the first chapter, we all suffer from a case of mistaken identity. What we identify as ourselves, the "I" is not the true Self or *Atma* but something else. This wrong understanding due to ignorance is what stands in the way of us realizing that we are happiness personified already. To attain happiness, all we need to do is remove the ignorance about who we are.

To accomplish this deviously simple sounding objective, we have to employ the next type of *yoga*. And that is *Jnana yoga*.

- 9 -

*J*NANA *Y*OGA

Jnana Yoga This is a course of discipline to gain knowledge. Knowledge of what? The subject of our study as we stated in the beginning is the Self, our self. As a brief preamble, I must mention here that in the interest of easy understanding, I will do my best to find the closest possible words in English for certain *Sanskrit* terms. They may not be the closest literal translation but rather the more meaningful translation.

The Self is referred to as *Atma*. The best term we can find for *Atma*, for now, is what most of us think of as the soul. So, we are seeking *Atma jnana*, knowledge of Self. And what is the purpose of gaining this knowledge? Gaining Self-Knowledge is the bridge that leads us to *moksha*. So, if we want to attain *moksha* or Liberation, we need Self-Knowledge. Not the knowledge about what we think is the Self, but the truth about our real Self. The truth in this case does indeed set us free.

How do we gain knowledge of anything? We do so by using an appropriate instrument of knowledge.

For example, if we want to know about color; what it is and what are the various colors etc., we need to use the appropriate instruments of knowledge, which in this case are our eyes. We cannot gain any knowledge about color if we refuse to use our eyes and want to use our ears or nose instead. If we want to gain knowledge of sound, we have to use the instrument of our ears and so on.

So, what instrument should we use to gain Self-Knowledge? For our everyday life, the main instruments we employ are those of perception (our sense organs) and inference (our brain or mind). Using these we gain knowledge of the world around us. When we want to learn about something, we direct the appropriate sense organs towards the object to be studied and based on the information thus gathered, the brain infers and converts it into knowledge. But the problem with this method is that all our instruments are extroverted, that is they face outward. This makes them well suited to gather information about the outside world. But they become quite useless when we want to gain knowledge about the Self or *Atma*, since that requires instruments that can look inwards.

It is easy to see how the sense organs are extroverted, but the brain can surely see within? No. We will see as we go on further, that compared to the *Atma*, the brain is still "outside" and outward facing. So how can we study the Self? Our eyes see everything but unfortunately, they cannot see themselves. So how do we see and study our eyes?

We use a mirror. So, an external object has to be recruited to study the eyes, even though the eyes can see and study everything. Similarly, to study the Self we need an outside object to be brought in. This also demands a certain humility in accepting that we need help to acquire the knowledge we so desperately seek. That outside thing is the scriptural teaching/teacher. A story is often recited to illustrate this point.

Once a learned teacher sent his disciples out into the village to gather their food. On their way back, there was a river they had to cross, and they had to cross it by wading in the water. The river was quite swift, and the water would often be high. The teacher warned them to be careful and entrusted their safety to the most senior disciple and asked him to make sure that all the men came back safely.

The disciples completed their tasks in the village and made their return journey. After crossing the river, the senior disciple wanted to be sure that they were all accounted for. So, he made all of them stand in a line and he counted them. No matter how many times he counted, he found only 9 men. One man was missing.

He was most distraught and repeated the exercise with many variations but to no avail. He could never find the missing man. He felt he had let down their teacher who had placed so much trust in him. When they all stood there dejected, who should appear there but their teacher himself.

He heard what had transpired and consoled the senior disciple.

"Do not worry. I will bring back the missing man."

"How will you do that, my teacher? What kind of sacrifices and austerities do we have to do? How long will it take master?" said he in tears.

"I will bring him back in an instant, without you having to do anything at all." said the master.

"Now go back and stand next to your brothers."

The master then counted the men and there were 10.

The senior disciple had failed to count himself when he had done the head count! No matter in which order he counted, he always failed to count himself.

But the teacher could see immediately that 10 men were present and accounted for.

It is the same when it comes to seeking knowledge of the Self. It is like the missing man in the story. The Self is always present but like the senior disciple, we do not see it and hence seek it everywhere else. But to the master, an entity who has the knowledge about the situation and the error being made, the answer is clear. This external entity is the scriptural teaching taught by an adept or a qualified teacher. The teachings and/or the teacher act as the mirror that we resorted to when we wanted to study our eyes.

- 10 -

STAGES OF STUDY

When we have made up our mind that our goal is to attain *moksha*, after ensuring that we are adequately qualified for this journey by employing *Karma yoga* and *Upasana yoga*, we stand at the threshold of *Jnana yoga*. Due to the vast amount of information that has to be imbibed, (although we will be seeing only a condensed portion of it), we need a plan of action that will make this manageable. We shall start by understanding how we are to take in the knowledge imparted by *Jnana yoga*. We can look at the entire process in three different stages, *Shravanam, Mananam* and *Nididhyasanam*.

Right now, let us not get dispirited by the *Sanskrit* names. Instead let us focus on them simply as stages I, II and III.

Shravanam (Stage I)

Shravanam is continuous, systematic studying of the teaching. Why continuous? We cannot do a few pages now and then forget all about it and come back a few months later and do a few more pages. Although there is no rule against it, this is not an effective way to learn any subject. Constant, everyday learning is a small but important step. Why systematic? Like building a house, the foundation has to be laid down first and then the walls are raised before building windows, stairs etc. It is impossible to do the windows first then do the foundation and then the walls. Similarly, we cannot simply see one lecture on youtube because we like that topic and then study a few pages from another book and then see another video and hope to build a correct and complete understanding of the topic. Again, there is no rule against it, but it will only make an already difficult task more difficult.

During the period of *shravanam*, usually questions are not allowed. Here again humility is expected; the humility to give the benefit of the doubt to the scripture and just try to understand as much of it as possible. Patience and faith are required to listen to the teaching without questioning. How is that possible? It is only natural that questions will arise when we study new material. Yes, this is true. But the practice of *shraddha* which we saw in the six-fold discipline should make this possible. This is one reason why *shraddha* is an area to strengthen during the preparatory phase. And if we did not possess this qualification, let us recollect the remedy. We were advised to follow one of the 3 *yogas* whenever we were lacking in a particular prerequisite. (*pg. 51*) And if the qualification we seek is one of the six-fold disciplines, (*shama, dama, uparama, titiksha, **shraddha**, samadhana*), then we have to practice *Upasana Yoga*. (*pg. 51*)

Mananam (Stage II)

In the *mananam* stage, we try to connect all the dots, so to speak. We arrange all that we have learned into one cohesive concept. When we do systematic study, taking small bites, chewing, and digesting them, things look clear. But when we try to "put it all together", we may run into seemingly contradicting facts, concepts that do not seem to "gel" with one another etc. This is fairly common in the study of any advanced subject. These apparent inconsistencies have to be analyzed and interpreted in the right context. Each and every piece has to be understood with thoroughness and then fitted together until all inconsistencies are resolved.

Mananam is the stage in which we have to question everything that isn't clear, and we have to clarify all doubts. Every question is encouraged. Since doubts arise in the domain of the intellect, *mananam* is an intellectual exercise. During the previous stage, *shravanam*, we were asked to only imbibe the knowledge. Here we are asked to analyze it and understand it thoroughly. The end result is to say with firm understanding and the resulting belief, "I am *Brahman*, I am eternal and all pervading" (For now do not worry about what these statements mean and how we make such claims.) So, *shravanam* removes ignorance and *mananam* removes doubts.

NIDIDHYASANAM (STAGE III)

This is the last stage. It is the process of assimilation and internalization of the *jnana* or knowledge. This is the actual application of the knowledge in our day to day life. It involves changing those actions born out of habituation and a lifetime of conditioning. We are now asked to look at our physical and emotional problems in light of the newly acquired *jnanam* (knowledge).

Although *samsara* (*pg. 41*) is basically a problem of ignorance, the ignorance manifests itself as emotional problems and turmoil.

We never say, *"I am unhappy because I am ignorant."*

We always say, *"I am unhappy because I am angry, because I am jealous, because I feel betrayed etc."*

Although at the fundamental level, the problem may be our own ignorance, we experience that ignorance in the various forms it takes. Ignorance sometimes assumes the shape of our likes and dislikes. At other times it colors our entire inner world with anger, greed, or jealousy. It may even take hold of us in the form of delusion and fear. All these are emotional manifestations of ignorance. This core of ignorance about who we are, is what is removed by *jnana* (knowledge). But there is no point in knowing and claiming, "I am all pervading, eternal *Brahman*", while continuing in our habitual pattern of complaining, getting worried or angry.

In *nididhyasanam* or stage III, we have to de condition ourselves, undo the emotional habits of a lifetime. We have to retune our thoughts in light of the teachings of *Vedanta* studied and clarified during *shravanam* and *mananam* respectively. When this is done, it translates into emotional strength.

Shravanam and *Mananam* and *Nididhyasanam* together result in *Jnana Yoga*. And this *Jnana Yoga* will give Self-knowledge. And as mentioned earlier Self-knowledge in turn will lead us to *moksha*. *Moksha* means,

"I am free in the presence and absence of things and people. I am free in my life and I am free even in death". This is achieved through *Jnana Yoga*, the subtlest form of knowledge and discipline.

Part II

– 1 –

SATYA AND MITHYA

In my own studies, the concept we are about to discuss was hard for me to grasp. We will keep revisiting this from many angles as we go on because it requires repeated learning. In this section we will start to familiarize ourselves with the idea of the real and the apparently real.

The cornerstone of knowledge is to understand the nature of reality. In order to do this, we have to recognize what is *satya* and what is *mithya*. This is the crux of *Tattvabodha*, called *tattva viveka*. *Tattva viveka* means the discriminative knowledge of truth. This is encapsulated is the following statement:

Atma satyam, tadanyat sarvam mithyeti

This means: *Atma* is *satya* (truth, real), other than that all else is *mithya* (only apparently real).

I have simply thrust the two words, *satya* and *mithya* in the previous paragraph with no explanation at all. Let us now dive into these two words, *satya* and *mithya*. First of all, it is important to grasp that these two words are not descriptions of objects, but rather they denote our understanding of objects. For example, when we point to a chair and say this is *satya* or *mithya*, it is not as a direct description (for example, this chair is black, or this chair is heavy). When we point to the chair and say this chair is *satya* or *mithya*, we are referring to our understanding of the chair as *satya* or *mithya*. It says that we have understood the nature of the chair to be *satya* or *mithya*. Hopefully, this will become clear as we proceed.

In very simple terms, *satya* means real or true. *Mithya* is something that is apparently real, kind of opposite of *satya* (for our purposes).

Let us use a park bench as an example.

If I ask, *"Is this bench real?"*

You will say, *"Yes. Of course, it is real."* So yes. The bench is *satya*.

Then I ask, *"What about the wood this bench is made of? If I call this whole object as the bench, where is the wood? Is it outside the bench?"*

You say, *"No."*

"Is it inside the bench?"

"No. But yes kind of… "

"So where is the wood?"

Wood is a different thing, another object, with its own description. Wood, which is different from wrought iron, plastic, aluminum, and other materials a bench can be made out of.

So now we have two objects, an object called bench and another object called wood.

I ask, *"Are they two separate objects?"*

"No," you say.

OK. Now I ask, *"If this bench weighs 10 pounds, is it the weight of the bench or the weight of the wood?"*

You think for a while and say, *"It is the weight of the wood."*

"So, does that mean that the bench has no weight?"

You say, *"No, the bench has a weight but… wait, the 10 pounds is the weight of the bench."*

"But you said just now that the weight belongs to the wood."

That doesn't sound right either. What shall we do?

We have to go about understanding this in the following way. The wood is the reality of the bench, there is only wood, there is no bench at all. But we cannot say that all there is, is wood alone. The wood is not a randomly thrown together pulpy mass. It has a certain shape and form and function. So how shall we view the bench in terms of its reality? Is it *satya*?

No, it cannot be true or real (*satya*) because it has no weight of its own. Yet, it is not nonexistent. Nonexistent things are objects that do not exist, like the hand of a horse. If I asked you, *"What's the weight of a horse's hand?"*, you could say with confidence that the weight is zero. For now, we can take anything that has this "zero weight" of its own, to be non-existent. Although our bench cannot be accorded its own weight, it is not like the "zero weight" situation of the horse's hand.

Something solid like a bench must have some weight. But as we have just seen, it does not; yet it is tangible. Therefore, we see that the tangibility and the weight of the bench belong to the wood and not to the bench. But we are in need of a term to describe this object (bench) whose reality is made up of wood. We call it a bench as opposed to something else made of wood like a chair or a table. This conceded reality of the bench is called *mithya*.

What kind of reality is *mithya*? What exists depending on another thing is called *mithya*. This is one way of understanding *mithya*.

Let us look at another example. I have a burger in my hand.

"Is it real or not?"

"Real."

Now I point to this and ask you what it is. You say it is a bun. If I call it a burger you will not accept it because it is a bun. But I want to find out where the burger is. I point to the next thing. That also is a bun, not a burger. I am getting a bit frustrated. I think let me go to the heart of the matter and I point to this. You say that it is called a patty, it is not a burger. This is a tomato, this is a lettuce, this is cheese and so on.

At the end of this, we are left staring at some pieces of bread, some meat, and some vegetables on a plate. So where is the burger now? Well, nowhere really. But we cannot say that there was no burger. There was a burger (before we pulled it apart!) what kind of burger? A *mithya* burger.

Now we understand *mithya* from another angle. It is something that is put together. When we say the burger is *mithya*, we are not dismissing it. It cannot be dismissed as non-existent, but neither can it be said to be self-existent. Being non self-existent, it has to depend upon something(s) for its existence. At the same time all these individual objects like patty, bun, lettuce, etc. are not just randomly thrown in a pile and called a burger. They are arranged in a systematic way to make a burger. But in reality, there is no burger, only an intelligently arranged set of objects. We can look at many things this way. For example, a car, a house, a family etc.

Let us look at a shirt. By now we are getting the hang of this, so the shirt is *mithya* and the fabric is *satya*. We say this because the shirt depends on the fabric to exist without which it has no independent existence. But what is fabric? Is it really *satya*? Is it self-existent? If something is *satya* it should exist by itself and not depend on another thing. But fabric is not self-existent, it depends on the yarn. Now fabric is *mithya* and the yarn is *satya*. But what is yarn? It is only made of fibers, without which it cannot exist. So, yarn is *mithya* and fiber is *satya*. And if we keep going on, we go down to the level of molecules and atoms. Then into the nucleus of the atom and electrons. And now we are at the level of particles. This particle is *satya*. Now if there is something on which this particle depends, then that will be *satya* and everything else above that level will be *mithya*. Each and every object we see, and experience can be dissected down to this level.

At that subatomic particle level, as science tells us we are talking in terms of concepts rather than objects. And concepts are cognized by consciousness, which is not an object. Consciousness is actually the substratum of everything. In fact, physicists tell us that in the world of the very small, all laws of Newtonian physics are suspended. The universe at that level functions per the seemingly unbelievable rules of quantum physics. And in the world of subatomic particles (which is the level we have gone into, with our shirt example), consciousness of the observer plays the crucial role. We will come back to consciousness and its role again in depth.

The difference between *satya* and *mithya* is this: *Satya* can exist without anything, but *mithya* depends on *satya* for its existence. Anything that depends on something else is *mithya* and what can exist on its own is *satya*.

So, since we can show that everything, we see in turn depends on something else, then is everything we see only mithya, meaning only apparently real?

Yes, it is true. And it is a rather disturbing thought. But we have to keep in mind that whenever we recognize something as *mithya*, we have to infer that *satya* is also present. Because without *satya*, there can be no *mithya*. So, we should not be dejected when confronted with *mithya*. We only need to have the *viveka* (discrimination) to look for the *satya* that is behind the *mithya*. Again, *mithya* or satya does not define the bench or burger or shirt, it refers to our understanding of the bench, burger, and shirt. We understand the bench, burger, and shirt to be *mithya*.

At the end of this discussion, we have reduced most of reality into objects and their subatomic particles and beyond that we have conceded that what exists is only consciousness.

– 2 –

DEFINITION OF *ATMA*

Let us now attempt to understand Consciousness. This is no easy task, and this will take us deep into the core teachings of *Vedanta*. From here we shall start following the trail of breadcrumbs that will ultimately lead us to Self-Knowledge.

What is *Atma*?

Tattvabodha defines *Atma* as, "The one who is distinct from the Gross, Subtle and Causal bodies, who is beyond the five levels (layers or sheaths) of experience, being the witness of the three states, that which remains in the form of existence, consciousness and fullness, that is the Self, *Atma*."

The above statement introduces a lot of new terms, which we need to understand if we are to fully grasp the meaning of *Atma*. We will go into all of them at length and soon we will be at ease with these terms. The three bodies, the five sheaths, the three states are all often mistaken for *Atma*. So *Tattvabodha* clarifies that, that which is none of the things mentioned above but is the witness of those things is the *Atma*.

Of all the things mentioned in the definition of *Atma*, the first one is the "three bodies". This is called "*Sharira Trayam*". *Sharira* means body and *Trayam* means three. Each and every living entity possesses not one but three bodies. This may sound a bit strange at first, but it is intriguing. It does not mean that we each possess three separate physical bodies. It means that in addition to what we see on the outside as the physical body, we have two other bodies. This is what we shall look at now.

When we want to study the structure of an organism or animal, we study its anatomy. When we want to know its functioning, we study its physiology. Knowing the anatomy and physiology can almost always give us a very good picture of the organism we are studying. We will approach the human being from a similar point of view.

Let us start with the anatomy first. For those of us who have studied anatomy, we will be familiar with the concept that we can look at the anatomy of the same organ in many different ways. The brain for example can be anatomically divided into cerebrum, cerebellum, medulla oblongata. It can also be divided into forebrain, mid brain, and hind brain. The latter is still an anatomical classification, but from a different angle. We study the anatomy from different perspectives depending on what point of view we are trying to understand.

Similarly, the first perspective of seeing the human body is as being made up of three bodies- *Sharira Trayam*.

These three are the Gross body, the Subtle body, and the Causal body. We will learn about all 3 of them in detail. In order to better understand it, we will organize the information about each body along these 4 aspects.

- the material it is made of
- its components
- its nature
- its function

– 3 –

THE GROSS BODY

THE GROSS BODY OR *STHULA SHARIRA*

The physical body that we touch, and feel is what we can call the Gross body. From here on when we say Gross body, we are referring to this physical body.

- **Material**: What is the material that makes up the Gross body?

In all ancient Indian sciences, be it *Ayurveda* (system of health), *Vaastu* (architecture) or *Jyotish* (*Vedic* astrology), the building blocks of matter are the 5 great elements or the *panchamahabhutas* (*pancha* is 5, *maha* is great, *bhutas* mean elements). These 5 elements are Ether/Space, Air, Fire, Water and Earth. In fact, everything in the universe that is of a material nature is made of these same 5 elements in various different permutations and combinations. So, our Gross bodies are also made up of the *panchamahabhutas*.

In our physical body, the Ether element is present wherever space is present, like in the bones, ear canal etc. The Air element is present in our air-filled organs like the lungs and intestines. Our body's temperature is the Fire element. The Water element is what makes up most of our physical body and what gives it shape. The Earth element gives our body the weight and bulk through muscles, fat etc.

- **Components**: What are the components of the Gross body?

We can enumerate each and every part but that is neither needed nor practical. For ease it is divided into head, arms, legs, and central part/trunk.

- **Nature**: What is the nature of our Gross body? Its main nature is change. It changes and undergoes transformation. It goes through 6 stages of transformation. They are as follows.

    Asti – The first state is the potential existence in the womb of the mother.

    Jayate – This the next change, which is birth.

Vardhate – Once the body is born, it starts growing.

Viparinamate – Metamorphosing i.e. growth has stopped but modification or changes continue. After the child becomes an adult, the body remains an adult body and does not grow further but undergoes various modifications.

Apakshiyate – This is the stage when it ages, grows old, and decays.

Maranam – Death of the body after which we cannot keep the body for long as it will start decaying in the true sense.

These various stages it undergoes is the inherent nature of the Gross body. Another characteristic of the Gross body is that it has a limited natural life. When it reaches the 6th stage (*maranam*), it ceases to exist.

My Gross body is visible and available for interaction to me as well as to others. What we mean by this is that I can see, feel, touch it and so can others; they can see, feel, and touch my body. By that account, I can also see, touch, and feel another person's Gross body.

- **Function:** What is the function of the Gross body?

This is the important part. The Gross body is the temporary abode used by the individual. It is like a rented home. Just like we stay in a rental property for a predetermined duration of time, we reside in our Gross body for as long as we live. What acts as the rent for this stay? *Karma.* The rent is based on our *karma*, both good *karma* (*punya*) and bad *karma* (*paapa*). As long as there is *karma* waiting to fructify, we inhabit this house. Once the allotted *karma* for this lifetime is done, there is no need for this Gross body, and we vacate the house.

Therefore, the Gross body is only a temporary residence we stay in, from where we transact with the world around us.

	Material	Composition	Nature	Function
Gross Body	5 great elements	Head, arms, legs, trunk	• Change • Short lifespan (usually <100 years) • Objective, visible to others	To interact with the outside world

Table 1. The Gross body

Why do we need to be aware of the Gross body from a *Vedanta* perspective?

We need to see it for what it is because this is what many of us take to be as the "Self". When we say, *"I am walking, I am eating, I am crying"*, we are referring to the Gross body that is doing all these actions. And the "I" referred to in these statements refers only to the Gross body, but we take that "I" to be the real "I". This is the first level of confusion, mistaking the Gross body for the Self.

The Gross body is *mithya*.

Why?

It is mithya because it cannot exist on its own.

If a fully formed and intact Gross body is lying on the bed, but does not have anything else, it is called a dead body or a corpse. It is nothing without whatever that it depends on to "be alive". By our previous explanation of *satya-mithya*, we can now see that the Gross body is *mithya* (because it cannot exist on its own and also because it is an intelligently put together collection of many parts).

Here let is stray a bit further to understand the concept of ownership and identity.

I point to your leg and ask, *"What is this?"*

You will say, *"This is my leg."*

I move on and point to your eye and ask the same question.

You will say, *"This is my eye, this is my face, this is my hair and so on"*

Now I point to your shirt and ask, *"What is this?"*

You will say, *"This is my shirt."*

Now comes the kicker. So, when you say, *"This is my shirt,"*

"Do you take the shirt to be you?

"No."

Whenever we say, *"This is my shirt, my car, my house,"* we mean to say that we are the owner of this object. We do not say that we are this object. We know the distinction. We know the difference between *"this is me"* and *"this is mine"*.

Yet, when we say, *"This is my head, this is my chest, this is my body,"* we take it to mean, *"This is me, this is I."*

What a strange thing!

So, whenever we own/possess a thing and say this is mine, automatically there exists an entity that "owns" and an object that is "owned". The very appearance of "my or mine" indicates that it is not me, it is only an object I own. I am distinct from that object.

Now when we look at our body, it should be clear that we are not the body. *The body is mine and the body is me, but I am not the body.*

~ 4 ~

THE SUBTLE BODY

THE SUBTLE BODY OR *SUKSHMA SHARIRA*

The second body we look at, is the Subtle body, also called the energy body or *Sukshma Sharira* (*Sukshma* means subtle or hidden, *sharira* is body)

- **Material**: The Subtle body is also made up of 5 elements. But these are the subtle form of the same *panchamahabhutas*. They are the subtle Ether/Space, subtle Air, subtle Fire, subtle Water, and subtle Earth. It is also material in nature like the Gross body.
- **Components & Function**: What are the components of the Subtle body?

There are 19 components to the Subtle body. They are the 19 instruments of experience.

The first set is the set of 5 *jnanyendriyas* (instruments of knowledge or sense organs). An *indriya* is an instrument. These are the eyes, ears, tongue, nose, and skin. When we say eyes, we do not mean the actual organ called the eye, we mean the power of vision, the organ that gives us the power of vision. Similarly nose here does not mean the anatomical nose (that is part of the Gross body), we mean the power of smell (which is part of the Subtle body).

These 5 *jnanyendriyas* (instruments of knowledge) help us sense the world around us. They are the subtle instruments of perception, through which we know the outside world.

Figure 2. The 5 Jnanendriyas (Instruments of Knowledge)

The next set is the set of 5 *karmendriyas* (instruments of action or motor organs). They are the organs of action. They are speech, hands, feet, excretory and reproductive organs. Again, feet do not refer to the actual physical feet with its bones, muscles, and skin. Those belong to the Gross body. Here we refer to the power of locomotion, which belongs to the Subtle body, that enables locomotion of the feet. I try to understand them as parts of the energy body versus parts of the Gross body. The physical hands with its bones and blood and skin as belonging to the Gross body and the actual hands that bring about action as belonging to the energy body.

Figure 3. The 5 Karmendriyas (Instruments of Action)

The next set in the components of the Subtle body is the set of 5 *pranas* (the life force). All the Gross body parts as well as the Subtle parts are animated by the life force called *prana*. *Prana* is sometimes equated to oxygen. But that is not strictly true. Life force is the closest translation. It is what carries the energy of life around the body. If someone is dead, pumping oxygen into them will not make them come alive. They will remain dead since they no longer have *prana*. It is the very minimum requirement for life. There are 5 subtypes of *prana* each performing a specific life sustaining function.

- *Prana-* is the force of the respiration that moves air through inhalation and exhalation. (Yes, *prana* is the name of the first subtype of *prana*, the life force.)
- *Vyana-* is the force of circulation, that pumps the blood from the heart to the rest of the body in a centrifugal fashion.
- *Samana-* is the force behind digestion. It powers the digestion of food, extraction of the nutrients and their assimilation.
- *Apana-* is the force behind the excretory function. It controls the throwing out of wastes from the body, in a downward direction.

- *Udana-* is the force of reversal, like vomiting out of unwanted or harmful substances. This is also responsible for speech and expression. It is said that *Udana* is the force that helps eject the Subtle body from the Gross body at the time of death.

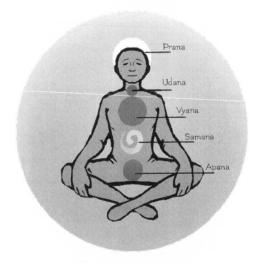

Figure 4. The 5 Pranas

The next set is the set of 4 internal instruments (*antakarana*). These 4 are the mind (*manas*), the intellect (*buddhi*), memory (*chitta*), and the ego (*ahamkara*).

- *Manas:* This is the seat of the emotional faculty, where emotions arise and are sifted. It is sometimes called the "heart" (as opposed to the "head"). It is also responsible for the doubting ability or the vacillation between two things. *Should I do this or that? Should I buy it or not?* It also functions to relay the messages from the intellect to the organs of action.

- *Buddhi:* This is the intellect, the discerning function. It is the rational faculty, the judging faculty, or the reasoning faculty.

The intellect gathers knowledge, discriminates, analyzes, and enquires into problems. From the enlightenment perspective intellect is the most important aspect of the Subtle body since Liberation is nothing but removal of ignorance from the intellect.

- *Chitta:* This is memory. Every input from the sensory organs and action is stored in the memory. Scriptures say that we have stored memories of experiences and faculties from even our past lifetimes. This is used to explain how child prodigies in music or sport seem to already "know" music or their sport before being taught.
- *Ahamkara:* This is the ego. Now the word ego has been used and misused in so many different

ways that it is very difficult to point to which meaning of the word is referred to in *Vedanta*.

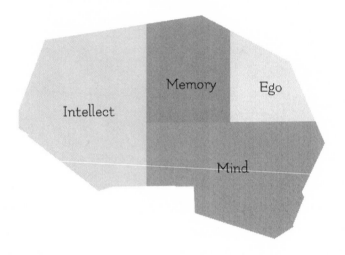

Figure 5. The 4 Antakaranas (Internal instruments)

So, in the next section, we will try to understand the ego (*ahamkara*).

— 5 —

THE EGO (*AHAMKARA*)

According to *Vedanta*, we can define ego as follows. Awareness/Consciousness seemingly forgets its limitless nature and identifies with the Subtle and Gross Body, and creates a secondary, limited identity which it calls "I". This "I" is called the ego.

We need to spend some time here to clarify the concept of ego. Where does this concept of "I" come from? As very young children, we have no concept of identity. We can all relate to how charming it is to see a toddler refer to himself in the third person. This concept of a personal identity is something we develop as we grow, watch, and learn from the cues around us. Within a few years, all of us develop an automatic, reflexive sense of identity. This is what we mean by "I" and this perceived identity is called the ego. From a *Vedanta* perspective there are a few aspects to understand.

- *Jiva*: A *jiva* is any entity which has the three bodies (Gross, Subtle and Causal). By that account all living things including human beings, animals and plants are *Jivas*. So, a *Jiva* has to first exist for it to have a sense of ego, the "I". Plants and animals, have this identity too. But in them, this faculty is not as highly developed as in humans.

- *Ahamkara (Ego)*: This is one of the 4 internal instruments, part of the subtle body. *Ahamkara* is not an independent volitional entity; it is simply the notion that "*I am a separate individual entity*", and the consequent belief that "*I am a doer and an enjoyer/experiencer*".

This internal instrument is the one who claims responsibility for all the decisions the intellect makes, and all the actions the mind and the body take.

In more specific terms, *Ahamkara* is the collection of ideas the individual has about himself such as "*I am male or female; I am black or white; I am fat, skinny, healthy, sick, artistic, business-minded, clean, etc.*"

- *Abhimana*: This is the third aspect which is an extension of *ahamkara,* and it involves possession. It is the sense of "This is mine". This is the closest definition to the ego in the western world. It is the sense of pride in the ownership of both material and non-material things. When used in a negative light it is close to conceit and arrogance and when used in a positive light, it is called pride. This may be about the possession of wealth (material things) as well as pride about one's superior intellect or skills, creativity, physical attributes, personal experiences and accomplishments (non-material things).

All of the above are part of the *Vedanta* definition of Ego. With these attributes, the *Jiva* identifies itself as the Ego and thinks it is the "doer" of these actions and the "enjoyer" (or sufferer) of the attributes.

We need *ahamkara* in order to function in this world. In our everyday lives we function in what is called "an apparent dualistic reality". What does this mean? Dualistic means anything that is in twos. In simple terms, we see the world in twos; black and white, good, and bad, right, and wrong. This dualism is one of the key elements that makes us live and function as we do. The most important aspect of this dualism is "I" versus the "rest of the world" or "I" versus "all the other things/persons" that is "non-I". So, it comes down to "me" versus "non-me". This is the dualistic reality we live in. We wake up and go about our everyday lives completely identifying with ourselves, with our limited Ego "I", and transact with the world taking the world to be "non-I". But that is only apparently dualistic. Unfortunately, we take it to be real.

However, we need this Ego/*ahamkara* in order to live and succeed in this world. Again, *Vedanta* does not call for the destruction or eradication of the Ego. It asks us to understand what it is. We have to understand that it is another one of our internal instruments (like memory). It is the sense of possession or ownership. It is an incorrect sense of identity we have assumed, taking ourselves to be the mind-body-sense organ complex.

Moreover, we need a highly refined intellect and healthy sense of "I" in order to engage in effective Self-Inquiry, and make the discrimination between the Self and the "not-Self" that facilitates the assimilation of Self-Knowledge and the "attainment" of ultimate inner freedom.

Ironically, we need the ability to effectively operate the mind-body-sense organ complex, in order to eradicate our identification with it. Our sense of being an apparent individual person is not actually the problem. Suffering happens only when we believe the apparent person is real and take it to be one's true identity.

When we understand that we are whole, complete, perfect, pure, limitless, attribute-less awareness and that as such no apparent object or experience can enhance, diminish or otherwise affect our essential nature in any way, then we are free.

Through the instrument of the mind-body-sense organ mechanism that constitutes the apparent individual person we seem to be, we will still encounter the ups and downs that characterize the drama of life.

However, while the experience of pain and pleasure will persist, suffering ceases once and for all.

Our association with the mind-body-sense organ complex therefore need not and, for that matter should not, be eradicated. Self-Realization does not mean destruction of any of our existing faculties. It is our identification with the body-mind-sense complex that should be negated through the assimilation of knowledge.

In short, we need to convert our "identification" with the Ego to an "association". Because I can observe the Ego, I am "associated" with it, but since I am not the Ego, I should not "identify" with it.

– 6 –

THE SUBTLE BODY-CONT.

We digressed to look at the Ego component of the Subtle body.

And now, let us continue our study of the Subtle body.

- **Function**: The main function of the Subtle body is to engage in transactions. It deals with transactions; some are inputs, some are outputs, and some are internal transactions.
- **Nature**: What is the nature of the Subtle body?

Like the Gross body, the Subtle body is also subject to change. Hence, we see especially with age, the deterioration of intellect, memory, vision, hearing etc.

Another characteristic of the Subtle body is its lifespan. The Subtle Body has a longer life compared to the

Gross Body. The Gross Body exists for only one birth or one lifetime, maybe about 80-100 years. But the Subtle Body continues into future lives as well. We may move from one physical body to the next, but the Subtle body continues in every one of them. That is why we are able to sometimes remember past life events. The *karma* from past lives is also carried forward because of the continuity of the Subtle Body. The Subtle Body continues until the dissolution of the Universe (*Pralaya*) where it gets dismantled.

The third characteristic of the Subtle body is that it is visible only to me. Unlike the Gross body which is available to others to touch/feel/see, my Subtle body cannot be seen/touched/felt by others. Only I can know my thoughts, my emotions etc. This is why it is called the Subtle body.

	Material	Composition	Nature	Function
Gross Body	5 great elements	Head, arms, legs, trunk	• Change • Short lifespan (usually <100 years) • Objective, visible to others	To interact with the outside world

Subtle Body	Subtle form of the 5 great elements	• 5 instruments of knowledge • 5 instruments of action • 5 pranas • 4 internal instruments	• Change • Longer lifespan (till the Destruction of the Universe) • Subjective, available only to me, not to others	Process transactions, inputs, outputs, and internal transactions

Table 2. The Subtle body and Gross body

Now let us talk about why we need to know about the Subtle body.

Previously when we learned about the Gross body, we concluded by saying that many of us wrongly think we are the Gross body.

Let me ask you, *"Of all the different parts of both the Gross and Subtle bodies we have seen so far, which do you take to be you?"*

Take a minute to think about it. There are some of us who already know that we are not the physical body. But let us take a step back and look at the world around us.

We see people who are attached to their worldly possessions; some to the extent that they take those possessions to be them. Those material goods and the trappings they bring are what they take to be their identity.

"Without this power, without this wealth, without this position in the world, I am nothing. I cannot afford to lose this…" and so on.

These people may also aspire to positions of leadership be it political, organizational, even familial. And this sense of identity is reinforced. Either they strive to achieve those possessions at all costs or if achieved they try to hang on to them at all costs. Anything that threatens that sphere must be fought and vanquished.

I think of this set of people to be in the outermost circle.

Next come the people who are strongly identified with the physical/Gross body.

"My beauty, my hair, my perfect, healthy body, my strength, my endurance. That beautiful, attractive person, that is me. That perfectly sculpted athletic, slim body, that is me."

Anything that affects the above, affects them deeply. Of course, it does. Because they are inextricably associated with the physical body. They have taken their physical body to be their identity. Anything that could possibly take away from the beauty, health and so on feels like a threat to their very existence.

These are the people in the next circle.

If we have already realized that the outermost circle

of power, wealth position etc. will come and go and that is not what "I" am and if we have also already realized that the next circle, the physical attributes of beauty, strength and health are not "me" then we now come to the next circle. This is where confusion most commonly occurs.

Of the 19 components of the Subtle body, the 4 internal organs (*antakaranas*) are what are often mistaken for Self or *Atma*. These 4 *antakaranas* are mind (*manas*), intellect (*buddhi*), memory (*chitta*) and ego (*ahamkara*). Let us start from the easy ones and go towards the harder ones.

Chitta or memory is often what makes us, us. Imagine if we had no memory. What a scary thought! We would have no identity. All the impressions and ideas we have of who we are will be gone in a minute. In short, we will be "lost". Although it is important, very few people identify themselves with their memory. Some may be proud of their memory/recall ability but the *antakarana* identified with in that case is the sense of possession (the Ego) of the memory faculty and not memory itself.

Manas or mind, the emotional headquarters, is what many of us identify with. I am a kind person, a gentle person, an angry person, a short-tempered person... these are some of the identities we assume for ourselves when we identify with our *manas*.

Buddhi or intellect is what is taken to be the Self by most people. This is especially true for analytical and academically successful people.

"Without my intellect, I am nothing. Anyone without a good intellect is a nobody." And so on.

But the majority of us end up believing the last *antakarana*, the Ego, to be "I".

"Without my skills, my superior intelligence, my excellent capabilities, I am nothing… ".

Some of us even go to the extent of saying,

"Without me, my wife/husband/family/team is nothing. I am the one that brings success to things. I am the doer, the enjoyer."

The 4 instruments, *manas, buddhi, chitta* and *ahamkara* are not 4 distinctly divided parts inside our anatomical brain. These are the functional aspects of the internal instruments of our Subtle body. Since they are part of the Subtle body, only I can access them. My thoughts, my emotions, my memories, and my Ego are available only to me. Unless I choose to exhibit them using my Subtle body and Gross body, they are private to me alone. How many times has it happened that we have had a certain understanding of a person's intentions or thoughts, sometimes even for years, before finally a heart to heart chat or through some other channel we come to know that we were wrong in our assumptions? For its vastness and powers, the mind can be fickle, the intellect can be short sighted, the memory is fallible, and the missteps of the Ego are too many to even mention. Yet even the most astute of us have chosen to identify ourselves with these 4.

As the individual or the *Jiva*, we choose any of the above components as our limited identity. We go about toiling in the world of *samsara*, facing the sufferings inherent in its setup. But the true or real "I" (which is the Self or *Atma*, which we will get to in later sections) is within us, unseen, unobserved, unrecognized.

There is a picture that is often used to demonstrate this rather unique set up. Perched on the branches of a tree are two birds. The tree is the tree of *samsara*. The two birds are identical to look at in all aspects. One bird is eating the fruits on the tree. The other bird is simply sitting still and watching the first bird. The first bird represents the *Jiva* or the individual. It is eating the fruits of the tree of *samsara*, just like we are. The second bird is the *Atma*. Unlike the first bird, it does nothing; it simply watches the first bird. For the *Atma* bird, the tree of *samsara* or its fruits are of no import. So, what is its purpose? It is what animates the *Jiva* or the first bird. Without the *Atma* bird, the other bird cannot exist. But the *Jiva* thinks he is the sole doer of everything and goes about his fruit gathering and eating jobs as if they are all important. He keeps himself busy, sometimes eating sweet fruits, sometimes eating sour fruits. The *Atma* bird knows about the *Jiva* bird but the *Jiva* bird remains in ignorance about the *Atma* bird. Yet they are identical birds, linked together and inseparable.

We have to learn to discern that "I" am not any of the 4 internal instruments. Again, they are me, but I am not them, be it *manas, buddhi, chitta* or *ahamkara*.

This is extremely hard to do. All our lives we have cultivated this identity, this Ego, this version of who we are. How can we let go? And if we do so then what do we replace it with? And most important of all how is this going to benefit me in my everyday life?

The benefit part is quite easy. Now that our mind has attained *viveka* and *viraga*, let us say my right ankle is injured in a fall from the stairs. It is very painful, might even be broken. My whole body is shaking with extreme pain. And the fear of what a broken ankle entails, takes hold. Very soon a flurry of scary thoughts and plans gone wrong swirl in my mind.

There is that important meeting at work which I cannot miss, otherwise those jackals will bypass me completely. Also, it is my right foot, how will I drive?

Then I also remember the past pain of the many needle sticks when I was in the hospital and the pain when they set my broken arm when I was a child. My neck has broken out in a sweat and I start to feel faint and disoriented. *Must be the pain.* I call out hoping someone will come to help me up. I curse myself for not keeping my phone with me at all times. At this moment, all my mistakes and follies seem to have caught up with me.

The actual injury is in reality a confined one; confined to my right ankle. It is an injury to one part of my physical body, nothing more. Yet I have managed to involve my entire being in this injury. My *manas* along with my *chitta* is conjuring up images of pain past and present and associated fears. My *buddhi* is trying to self-diagnose the injury and is calculating what aspects and actions of my life will be affected and how. My Ego is fighting and resisting these possible scenarios and is also blaming me for my mistakes past and present and adding to the fears of the *manas*.

It is almost as if my entire "brain" is working against me, making the situation worse instead of better.

Instead using *viveka*, if I can understand and isolate that only one very small aspect of my Gross body is all that is affected and if I can rein in my Subtle body including my *manas*, *chitta*, *buddhi* and *ahamkara*, things start to look a lot better. I can then harness my 4 internal instruments towards a solution. Also, I can stop the injury to one body part from turning into a disaster that has affected the entire "me". Please note that I have not said anything about pain. Of course, there will be pain from the injured ankle. Just because I have *viveka*, does not mean I have become immune to pain. That may be possible for some highly trained *yogis* but not yet for us beginners.

– 7 –

THE CAUSAL BODY

THE CAUSAL BODY OR *KARANA SHARIRA*

The third body we all possess is the Causal body or *karana sharira* (*karana* means cause). As the name suggests it is the cause of the other two bodies. This is again a concept that is particularly hard to grasp. We will use the same template as before to study the Causal body.

- **Material**: Since it is very subtle in nature it is made up of matter in its subtlest form. Technically it is made up of something called *avidya*. *Avidya* usually means ignorance but not in this context. In this context it is sometimes referred to as *Maya*. We will go into great depth about *Maya* later. (pg 199, pg 201)
- **Components**: *Karana sharira* is nothing but the Subtle and Gross body but in their seed form. The

Causal body is that from which the Subtle and Gross bodies are derived. To illustrate this point, here is an example. Think of a seed and a tree. We see the tree today with its branches, leaves, flowers, fruits etc. But 10 or 20 years ago, there was no tree. But the tree still existed- in a seed. If we open a seed and look for the tree, we will not find it. Similarly, if we take the tree apart and look for the seed that became this tree, we will not find that either. Within the tree's fruit we may find a seed, but it will be the seed for another new tree, not the current tree under study. The Causal body is like the seed from which the tree evolves. This fully grown tree in its own time will bear fruits which will contain seeds. When the tree dies, from its seed another tree sprouts.

- **Function**: What is the function of this Causal body? Its main function is to act as the storehouse for the other two bodies. During Creation (*Shristi*), it is the source from which the Subtle and Gross bodies arise (pg. 206) and during Destruction (*Pralayam*) the Subtle and Gross bodies dissolve back into the Causal body.

- **Nature**: The Causal body has the longest life span of the three bodies. The Subtle body is dismantled at the time of *Pralayam* (Destruction) at least. Here *Pralayam* is not destruction of the individual or death, it refers to the destruction of the entire universe, which is a very long time indeed. But the Causal body continues even beyond *Pralayam*. This is because nothing in this universe (including the universe) can be created or destroyed, they merely shift from one form to another. Matter is converted into energy at the time of destruction and energy is remade into matter at the time of creation. Think of the stars in the universe. Thousands of stars (matter) are born in the universe (from energy) and thousands of stars (matter) are also destroyed (explode releasing energy). So, matter is constantly being converted into energy during explosion and energy is condensed into matter when a new star is born. It is the same with us and the universe in its entirety.

Another important nature of the Causal body is that unlike the Gross body (which is perceived by both others and me) and the Subtle body (which can be perceived only by me and not others), the Causal body cannot be perceived even by me. So, neither others nor I can perceive the Causal body. Why? Although the Causal body is made up of matter (just like the Subtle and Gross body) the matter it is made up of is of the subtlest nature, even more subtle that our mind/intellect (which belongs to the Subtle body). In other words, a less subtle object cannot perceive a more subtle object. Therefore, the intellect/mind (belonging to the Subtle body) cannot perceive the extremely subtle Causal body.

	Material	Composition	Nature	Function
Gross Body	5 great elements	Head, arms, legs, trunk	• Change • Short lifespan (usually <100 years) • Objective, visible to others	To interact with the outside world
	Material	Composition	Nature	Function
Subtle Body	Subtle form of the 5 great elements	• 5 instruments of knowledge • 5 instruments of action • 5 pranas • 4 internal instruments	• Change • Longer lifespan (till the Destruction of the Universe) • Subjective, available only to me, not to others	Process transactions, inputs, outputs, and internal transactions

Causal Body	Subtlest form of the 5 great elements	• Seed form of Subtle and Gross bodies	• Longest lifespan of the 3 bodies (continues beyond the Destruction of the Universe) • Unavailable even to me	Acts as the storehouse for the Subtle and Gross bodies

Table 3. The Causal body, Subtle body and Gross body

Here, we will digress once again into a topic called *vasanas*. *Vasana* means a fragrance, like that of a flower. Even if we remove the flower from the place it leaves behind a subtle smell, a trace. This is called a *vasana*. Similarly, every experience we undergo generates a *vasana*. It could be a pleasant *vasana* from a joyful experience or an unpleasant one from a bad experience. For example, we have had a pleasant experience, maybe eating a particularly tasty dish. The experience is over, and we go about our business, but it has generated a *vasana* in us. This is what stimulates us to go looking for the same experience again. In other words, this is what transforms into desire/wish/want.

Again, it is not a bad thing to have *vasanas*. We all have them, even the most realized *yogis*. As long as we are alive, we have *vasanas*. But to have binding *vasanas*;

now that is what causes problems. These lead to binding desires which force our actions, to acquire or to avoid experiences. We have discussed this earlier under binding desires (*pg. 36*).

Sometimes *vasanas* are distorted by the mind. A person may start eating, not to satisfy hunger or just to eat tasty food, but to satisfy emotions. This normal *vasana* for food is now distorted into a binding *vasana* for satisfaction.

Where are these *vasanas* located? Although they are part of the Subtle body, their seeds are really located in the *Karana Sharira*, in the Causal body, which is why we are discussing them in the context of the *Karana Sharira*. Since they are stored at the level of the Causal and Subtle bodies, they can be carried on into other births.

– 8 –

THE 5 SHEATHS

We have completed our very brief look at the 3 bodies, the *Sharira Trayam*. Now we move on to the 5 sheaths. Let us go back to the start of the *Sharira Trayam* discussion. The human entity can be studied from different perspectives. One such perspective was the concept of the 3 bodies. The 5 sheath or *panchakosha* (*pancha* is 5 and *kosha* is sheath) model if you will, is another angle of study. Since we have looked at the 3 bodies and are familiar with some of the basics, the 5-sheath model will be easier to grasp.

We can look at the human being as being made up of 5 sheaths. Sheaths are merely layers or coverings. They are conceptual layers, not to be taken as literal layers that can be peeled away by hand or instrument. Here is another way to look at it. The 3 bodies concept is a classification based on anatomy, study of structure and composition. For example, the *Sthula Sharira* is made of up gross matter, the *Sukshma Sharira* is made up of subtle matter and the *Karana Sharira* is made up of Causal matter. The 5-sheath model can be considered to be the physiology-based classification or function-based classification.

With that introduction let us look at the 5 sheaths. They can be visualized as concentric circles or as nesting dolls.

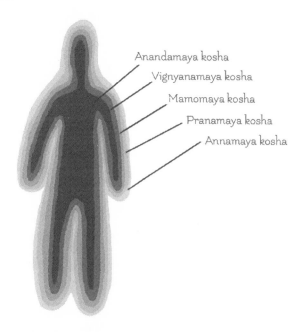

Anandamaya kosha
Vignyanamaya kosha
Mamomaya kosha
Pranamaya kosha
Annamaya kosha

Figure 6. The 5 Koshas (Sheaths)

From out to in, they are,

- Sheath I- *Annamaya kosha*: This is the food sheath or physical sheath. This belongs to the Gross body and is the outermost layer. It is an anatomical layer made up of the structure of our body, our limbs, organs etc. This is made from and nourished by food (called *annam* in Sanskrit) that we consume. Food is considered to be the grossest form of energy in the world.
- Sheath II- *Pranamaya kosha*: This is the vital or energy sheath. It is the physiological sheath. To reiterate, anatomy is the structure of the body and physiology is the function. *Pranamaya kosha* is part of the Subtle body or *Sukshma Sharira*. This sheath is what makes the body parts function by providing them with vital energy called *prana* which animates the organs.

This *kosha* consists of the 5 *pranas* (we discussed this earlier under Subtle body) and 5 instruments of action, the *karmendriyas*. The 5 *karmendriyas* are tongue/ speech, hands, legs, anus, and genitals. The *Pranamaya kosha*, made up of the 5 *pranas* and the 5 *karmendriyas*, is called

Kriya Shakthi or the power to create/action. This is because it has energy (*prana*) and tools (5 tools of action).

5 *pranas* (Energy) + 5 Motor organs (Tools)
= *Kriya Shakthi* (Action power)

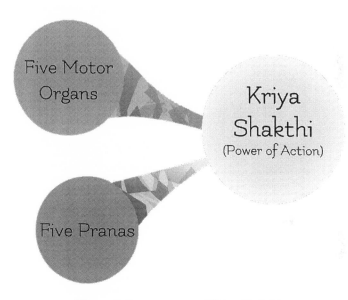

Figure 7. Components of Kriya Shakthi

The role of the *Pranamaya kosha* is better understood when we look at what happens at the time of death. When a person dies, his physical body (*Sthula Sharira* or *Annamaya kosha*) is left behind. But since the Subtle body has departed, taking the *Pranamaya kosha* (*Kriya*

Shakthi, the action power) with it, no action is possible by the Gross body that has been left behind. When organs (part of *Annamaya kosha*) from a recently dead person are transplanted into a living person, they can function because the *Kriya Shakthi* (*Pranamaya kosha*) of the recipient is present. This again illustrates that the Subtle body is needed for the Gross body to function.

- Sheath III- *Mamomaya kosha*: This is the Mind sheath. This belongs to the Subtle body and is also called the psychological sheath. Emotions, feelings, doubts and dealing with them reside in the *Manomaya kosha*. For the *Manomaya kosha* to do its work it has the following under it.

The 5 *jnanyendriyas* or sense organs or organs of knowledge (eyes, ears, tongue, taste, and touch) and 3 (mind, memory, and Ego) of the 4 internal organs (*antakaranas*). It works by gathering information about the outside world through the 5 sense organs and processes them in the mind (*manas*), memory (*chitta*) and Ego (*ahamkara*) parts of the 4 *antakaranas*. As you can see the intellect (*buddhi*) is not included in this *kosha*.

This is the sheath where all desires and wishes originate. This desire that motivates a *Jiva* (individual) to action is called *Iccha Shakthi* (power of desire).

5 Sense organs + Mind + Memory + Ego
= *Iccha Shakthi* (power of desire)

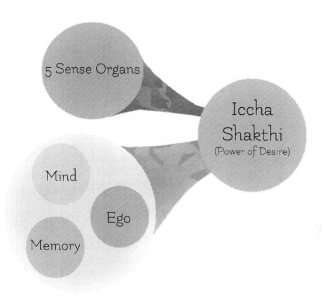

Figure 8. Components of Iccha Shakthi

Desire comes first. Then we act. So *Iccha Shakthi* pushes or prods *Kriya Shakthi* into action. This is how our wishes and desires are converted into action.

Let us digress a little here. This process of how desire

is converted into action is especially important to remember. We often think that we act randomly or on the spur of the moment or we do things without thinking. We believe that our actions, especially our less than noble ones, "just happen". Sadly, no. That is not the case. All action or *Kriya Shakthi* (the creating or acting power) has its source in *Iccha Shakthi* (power of desire). The root of all our actions is desire and our desires lead us into actions that will satisfy those desires. This is why desire is said to be the root cause of all evil. Excessive desire, which is unbridled, will lead to actions that satisfy those desires at all costs. But wait a minute, we do not act on all our desires. That is where we come to the next layer or sheath.

- Sheath IV- *Vignyanamaya kosha*: This is the Intellect sheath. It belongs to the Subtle body and is also called the cognitive sheath. In fact, *Pranamaya kosha, Manomaya kosha* and *Vignyanamaya kosha* together are part of the Subtle body.

All intellectual functions like reason, knowledge, judgement, discrimination are processed by the *Vignyanamaya kosha*.

The cognitive sheath consists of the 5 *jnanyendriyas* or sense organs or organs of knowledge (eyes, ears, tongue, taste, and touch) and 3 (*buddhi*, *chitta* and *ahamkara*) of the 4 internal organs (*antakaranas*). Using the information about the world gathered by the 5 sense organs, the *Vignyanamaya kosha* processes them through the intellect (*buddhi*), using memory (*chitta*) and Ego (*ahamkara*). This sheath with its components is called *Jnana Shakthi* (knowing power, power of or power from knowledge).

5 Sense organs + Intellect + Memory + Ego
= *Jnana Shakthi* (knowing power)

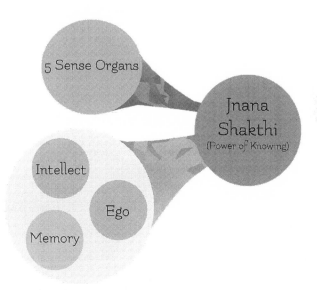

Figure 9. Components of Jnana Shakthi

In short, *Jnana Shakthi* knows/finds out/researches, *Iccha Shakthi* desires/wants/wishes and *Kriya Shakthi* goes forth and does/acts/acquires. This is the chain of events behind all action. We already saw how *Iccha Shakthi* triggers and controls the direction taken by *Kriya Shakthi*.

What is the role of *Jnana Shakthi*? This is our fail safe, our ultimate weapon which keeps *Iccha Shakthi* in check. Knowledge is what places a check on our desires. It almost acts like the supervisor for *Iccha Shakthi's* activities. This is why we do not act on every desire we have; because we know that it is not right/appropriate/acceptable etc.

If we are working at an *Iccha Shakthi – Kriya Shakthi* level, it is a fairly primitive way of functioning, like a baby or a child. I want it, I have to have it!

As we develop *Jnana Shakthi*, we learn to be discriminative in our desires. All these 3 *shakthis* (powers) are developed to different degrees in different people. By strengthening our *Jnana Shakthi*, we can guide our desires and actions better. This is why *manas* or mind is not part of the intellect/cognitive sheath, it belongs in the psychological sheath. And it is also why *buddhi* (intellect) is not part of the psychological sheath but belongs to the intellect sheath. *Chitta* (memory) and *ahamkara* (ego) belong in both. We need the memory bank to process both emotions and information and we need that important stamp of "I" for both desire and intellect. This is why memory and Ego belong in both the sheaths. We move on to the 5th sheath or the innermost sheath.

- Sheath V- *Anandamaya kosha*: This is the Bliss sheath. This belongs to the Causal body or *Karana sharira*. Let us recollect what we know about the Causal body. It is not perceived by either me or others. So, it is always a bit tricky. For ease of understanding, we can refer to it as the "unconscious" mind, as they say in psychology. This is where all our conditioning, our behavior and personality are present in their seed form. It is also where all unprocessed or incompletely processed thoughts, feelings and emotions are buried. Experiences too painful to deal with in the conscious state or painful/angry emotions that have not found an appropriate outlet are squirreled away in the unconscious mind. This explains why sometimes we have a very violent reaction to a very minor mistake/insult.

But why is the storehouse of all these violent and unsavory seeds of thoughts called the bliss sheath? Since it is not accessible to us (by this we mean our intellect, mind, memory, or ego), we are unaware of their existence. Whenever we are unaware of certain things, we are in a state of bliss as far as those things are concerned. This is why it is called the *Anandamaya kosha* (*ananda* means bliss). This unawareness, this ignorance is sometimes referred to as *avidhya*. This ignorance is an important substrate of the *karana sharira*. We shall learn more about this ignorance later.

Why do we need to know about these 5 sheaths? What is their role in Self-Inquiry? These 5 sheaths are coverings or *upadhis* for the Self.

What is an *upadhi*? It means "that which apparently lends its attributes to something else". So, each of the *koshas* is an *upadhi* for the Self. Suppose we have a clear crystal vase. Into this we pour cranberry juice. Because of the red color of the cranberry juice, the clear crystal vase will look to be a red colored vase. Now let us empty it out and pour orange juice into it. Now the same clear crystal vase will look yellow in color. The cranberry juice is an *upadhi* for the vase. The orange juice is another *upadhi* for the vase.

What we need to understand here is that when we poured cranberry juice into the vase, the crystal did not change its color, it apparently took on the color of the juice (only apparently because it really did not "take in" the red color). The crystal was always clear; in the empty state, with the cranberry juice in it (when it looked red), and with the orange juice in it (when it looked yellow).

Both the juices are *upadhis* for the crystal. The "redness" and the "yellowness" belong to the cranberry and orange juices respectively and not to the crystal. Similarly, the 5 koshas are *upadhis* for the Self. They do not change or hide the Self like a true covering. Just like the crystal did, the Self only apparently takes on the attributes of the *koshas*. This is true of the 3 bodies too. The Gross body, the Subtle body and the Causal body are also *upadhis* for the Self. They are mistaken for the Self when in fact they are only the outer coverings whose attributes we wrongly take to be those of the Self.

Here are some examples of how the *koshas* become *upadhis* for the Self.

At the level of the physical body we see experience as "I am a mortal", "I am fat", "I am short" and so on, which is a mistake. The body (*Annamaya Kosha*) apparently becomes an *upadhi* for the Self. The body is the Self, but the Self is not the body.

At the *Pranamaya kosha* (vital or energy sheath) level there is experience arising from the physiological functions of *prana*. This accounts for the experience of "I am hungry", "I am thirsty", "I am not healthy" etc. The "I" and *Prana* (Life force) are taken as identical. *Prana* is Self, but Self is not *Prana*.

At the *Manomaya kosha* (psychological sheath) level, the actions of the mind are taken to be the attributes of the Self. "I am restless", "I am angry", "I am sad", "I am afraid", are experiences at the level of the mind. Restlessness, anger, sadness, fear are states of mind, not the Self. Because again, mind is the Self, but the Self is not the mind.

At the level of the *Vijnanamaya Kosha* (intellectual sheath), the experience of "I am a thinker", "I am a doer", are mistaken for the Self.

At every level, we make the same mistake of identifying with the *upadhi* instead of the Self. Knowing the description of these *upadhis* and the distinction between them and the Self are an important part of *jnana yoga*. If we know ourselves to be the Self, we are freed from the experiences at the level of the 5 *koshas* and the 3 bodies. As long as we think of any or all of the *upadhis* as the Self, we will never be able to attain *moksha*.

- 9 -

THE 3 STATES OF EXPERIENCE

The third and last viewpoint of studying ourselves is through the 3 states of experience. This is called the *Avastha Trayam* (meaning three states). At any given time during the 24 hour cycle, we spend in one of these three states of experience. What are the 3 states? They are the waking state, the dream state, and the sleep state. As a *Jiva* or an individual we move from one state to the next and that is how we experience the world. We experience the world when we are awake, but also when we are dreaming and when we are in the sleep state. An important point to note is that when we say sleep state, we mean deep sleep with no dreams. In order to understand what is happening in these states let us study them methodically. We shall look at the following aspects in each of the 3 states.

- The condition of the mind, as the mind plays a prominent role in each state.
- The nature of experience
- The dominant medium in each state.

THE WAKING STATE

Let us start with the waking state. All of us are well aware of this state. This is our predominant state of experience. When we say "me" or "I", we are most commonly referring to the "I" in the waking state. This is the "I" we are thinking of that is a student or an employee, or a boss, a husband, a wife etc. This is the "I" that goes to work, earns money, plays mind games with friends, and has arguments with loved ones to name just a few. This is the "I", where Consciousness seems to forget its true limitless nature, and identifies with a limited "I" associated with the Gross and Subtle bodies. The waking state entity is Consciousness turned outward, shining through the senses, mind, and intellect.

Condition of the mind: In the waking state, the mind is fully operational, which means that all 4 internal organs are working. Ego, memory, emotions, and rational thought are all working. Since they are operational, the experiences associated with them, will be felt. Gathering new information and experiences through the intellect, filing them away for the future, using the memory, feeling sorrow, joy, fear, using the mind and "owning" them all through the Ego, will be experienced. As the waking state entity, we are consumers of experiences. We crave encounters and interaction, not necessarily with people. When I say encounter, I mean the meeting of our instruments, say our sense organs with their corresponding stimuli. We devour experiences through the sense organs, motor organs and the mind.

Nature of experience: In the waking state, we experience a world external to our mind-body-sense organ complex. And since it is an external universe, it is a concrete, tangible world of experience. We can feel it because it is made out of tangible matter. It is also an objective world. What this means is that the world we see, and experience is also available to others to see and experience. The waking world is experienced via the 5 sense organs, our eyes, ears, nose, skin, and tongue. The waking state is a two-way interaction. We receive information (via the sense organs) and we also perform action (via the motor organs).

On the whole, the waking state has the following qualities,

- It is concrete or tangible.
- It is objective.

- It is sense organ based.
- It is a two-way interaction.

Medium: Let us look at what the dominant medium of the waking state is. In order to experience the waking state, we need our sense organs. The waking state is a sense organ-based experience. For the sense organs to function, they need the corresponding physical organ (*pg. 105*). For example, the power of the sensory function of smell is part of the Subtle body. But in order to function, it requires the physical nose (which is part of the Gross body). So, the sensory powers require their corresponding physical parts in order to work.

Because we have to experience the external world, we need sense organs. To operate the sense organs, we need the body. Without the Gross Body, the physical world cannot be experienced. So, the Gross Body is said to be the dominant medium in the waking state.

For our current purpose, the waking state is not all that interesting, since we already are very familiar with it. Let us move on to the next state.

THE DREAM STATE

Unlike the waking state entity, where Consciousness shines outwards, in the dream state, Consciousness turns inwards and illuminates an internal world made up of our memories and *vasanas* (*pg. 130*). Like in the waking state where we believe that the world we experience is real, in the dream state we believe that the dream world is real. Our dreams are lit up by light even though the senses are inactive, and our eyes are closed. How do we "see" the dream? Who or what illuminates it? Consciousness shines through the dreamer, just as it shines through the waking state entity making it possible for us to "see" our dreams.

Condition of the mind: In the dream state, only the memory part of the mind is active. Everything we see, feel, and experience in our dream is simply a compilation of various memories. The images we see, the sounds we hear are all pulled from the sensory memory bank, the emotions we experience in dream state are pulled from the *manas* memory bank. Even the ego or the "I" we feel in dreams is only the memory of the waking "I", not a new or fresh "I". All that we experience when we are awake, gets recorded in our memory (*chitta*) and gets played back to us during sleep. It applies not just to the things we are actively trying to memorize like passwords or anniversaries. All data that is within our sphere, objects in our peripheral vision, sounds from the television playing in the background as we cook, new items that we scrolled past are all recorded irrespective of whether we want them in our memory or not. This is another reason to gain control over our sense organs as emphasized in the chapter on *Upasana Yoga* (*pg. 58*).

Nature of experience: The dream state is an internal state. It is created not outside of the dreamer but within him or her. In the dream state, the world we experience is subjective, which means that only we participate in it. Another person cannot see or experience my dream. Another unique nature of the dream world is that it is not concrete or tangible. It shifts and changes quickly and often without any logic. Now we are falling through a void and now we are riding a horse in a field, now we are eating an apple, all very seamlessly blending to make sense somehow. It is not something we can grasp with our sensory or motor organs. Therefore, unlike the waking world, the dream world has the following qualities,

- It is subjective.
- It is intangible.
- It is abstract.

Sometimes we see things in dreams that we have never seen in waking state, so how can that be from our memory? For example, a flying man. We have never seen a flying man during our waking state, so how can this be recorded in our memory and then be replayed in our dream? The flying man in the dream is simply the compilation of multiple memories (like the wings of a bird, body of a man, or even a memory from a sci-fi novel) meshed together to generate a new object that we may have never encountered as such in our waking state. Anything that we have consciously or subconsciously seen or experienced in our waking state can put in an appearance in the dream state, in whole, in part or in jumbled form. Books we read, movies we see, stories recounted by friends, even mundane daily activities form the sources for dreams. Our own wishes, wants, dislikes and aversions, fears, and mistakes that we experience in the waking state become candidates for appearing in the dream state.

An interesting question that arises is that in rare instances, in their dreams some people can see things that are yet to happen. If the dream world is entirely compiled from memory (that is the past, events that have already occurred) how can a person "see" things that are yet to happen (the future, which is not in the memory) in their dreams?

If a person sees future events, it is only a unique faculty of the mind which others have not developed, because coming events often cast their shadows ahead of their occurrence. This statement seems all mysterious. But let us think about things in a slightly different way. All events already exist in potential or seed form, just like all trees exist in seed form, many years before they become trees. Just like that, events yet to happen exist in their seed form somewhere in the fabric of space and time. When something is still in seed form, it is too subtle for us to understand. But if the mind is sensitized enough, it can "peek" into this world of potential events. *Yogis* deliberately develop this faculty. But in our case, this peeking into the future can sometimes happen by mere accident. This is why it is only a glimpse and the average person cannot describe too many details of a future event they have seen in their dream. So, to be accurate, this is not a dream but rather a vision, a quick glimpse by the sensitized mind into the potential universe of events.

Yet another interesting question is about instances where people remember events from their past birth, especially children. If we recollect, only the Gross body is destroyed in death. The Subtle and Causal bodies leave the Gross body and move on to another Gross body. We should recollect that *chitta* or memory is part of the Subtle body, and the Subtle body travels from one birth to the next. Since it is a sort of continuation from the previous birth it is possible for the memories of the past birth to be carried over. The *vasanas* residing in the Causal body can also be carried over and manifest in the present birth. *Vasanas* are those trace aftereffects of experience, like the fragrance left by a flower, even after the flower is removed. If a person had a bad experience in water in one birth, it creates a *vasana* in his Causal body. This Causal body (along with the Subtle body) transfers to the next birth. Now this child (in the new birth) may exhibit an abnormal fear of water from a very young age, even when nothing bad has happened to him in water in his current birth. No amount of coaxing can make this child get into the pool while other children laugh and clap with joy at the sight of water. We have all seen this happen in our neighborhood pools and at swim lessons. Transferred *vasanas* (both positive and negative ones) explain some of these phenomena especially in the case of children where memories/ *vasanas* of the present birth are still in the formative stage.

Medium: Let us look at the dominant medium of the dream state. In order to experience the dream state, we need only one of the 4 internal organs and that is the memory or *chitta*. And this belongs to the Subtle body. Therefore, the dominant medium of the dream state is the Subtle body.

THE SLEEP STATE

When we say sleep state, we mean the state of deep sleep, without dreams. This is the state about which we recollect nothing. This is also the state where we experience bliss. This is the state that writers/authors mean when they write, "*He fell into a dreamless sleep.*" And usually in the story, after waking up from this "dreamless sleep" the protagonist will have an epiphany or will find the courage needed to fight his enemies, slay the dragon, and win the princess and so on.

The sleep state is filled with happiness but where neither the external nor the internal world exists. In other words, Consciousness is directed neither outwards (as in waking state) nor inwards (as in dream state). Consciousness is formless and directionless in the sleep state.

The sleeper ego is extremely subtle, its presence indicated by the fact that we experience limitlessness and bliss. Occasionally we do find bliss in our awake state and dream state. However, in these two states, the bliss we find is sporadic. This is because in these two states, the bliss is interrupted by changes in thoughts and feelings. The thought or act that gave us the bliss changes and the feeling of bliss is gone. But in deep sleep it is continuous as there are no thoughts and feelings there to interrupt the bliss.

Condition of the mind: In deep sleep, the mind is almost completely dormant. So, internal organs (mind, memory, intellect, and Ego) are not active. The Subtle body is not functioning. Because of this there are no emotions (hence no sadness, fear), no memories, no ideas or thought processes, and no sense of "I". Even the sense of "I am sleeping" is not there at that moment. The entire Subtle body is as though it is dissolved into its seed form or into the Causal body.

The deep sleep state is the seed form for the other states. Depending upon the seed sprouting into the dream state or the waking state, we the *Jiva* become the dreamer or the waking state entity and experience the corresponding world.

Nature of experience: Since the Gross body is not working, there is no knowledge of the external world. Since the Subtle body is not working, there is no knowledge of the internal world. There is no concrete, tangible, objective external world and there is no abstract, intangible, subjective internal world to experience either.

Therefore, it is a state of complete self-ignorance. This is the nature of experience in the sleep state.

Medium: Since the Gross body and the Subtle body are not functioning, it is only the Causal body that is operational in the sleep state. It correlates with the seed-like state of experience. It is the subtlest state, so subtle it cannot be perceived and understood by our mind. This is very characteristic of the Causal body.

– 10 –

BACK TO THE DEFINITION OF *ATMA- NETI, NETI*

That ends our explanation of the 3 states of experience. Let us now go back to the origin, the reason for all the above explanations. We started out with the definition of *Atma*. It was in order to understand this definition that we had to study all that we did in the last few sections. Now let us look at the definition again.

Definition of *Atma*:

"The one who is distinct from the Gross, Subtle and Causal bodies, who is beyond the five levels (layers or sheaths) of experience, being the witness of the three states, that which remains in the form of existence, consciousness and fullness, that is the self, *Atma*."

From our studies, we can now understand the terms in the above definition. We know about the 3 bodies, we know about the 5 *koshas*, we know about the 3 states of experience. What this definition is trying to say is that the *Atma* is the not any of the above but is the witness of all the above. It also gives a few descriptive terms about what it is. We shall look into those a bit later.

When we set out to define and understand something, there are many ways of going about it. Negation is one way. This means to list the things something is not; *neti, neti* (not this, not this). We point to the things it is not. Suppose we want to tell our friend what a persimmon is, and he has never seen one. We have a fruit bowl with many fruits in them, including our persimmon. We point to the apple, the navel orange, the grapes, the passion fruit and keep saying not this, not this and then finally we come to the fruit that has not yet been pointed out, that is the persimmon. It is one way of telling someone what a persimmon is. You may say that is a roundabout way of telling someone what a persimmon is. Instead of pointing to all the other fruits and saying they are not persimmons, why not pick up the persimmon from the bowl, show it to the person and say, *"This here is a persimmon!"*?

Good point. Suppose it is not a persimmon we have

to educate someone about. Suppose we have to tell someone what a satsuma is. They have an idea that it is a citrus fruit, like an orange or a clementine. Now we could pick up a stand-alone satsuma and show them. Or we can fill a bowl with all possible similar looking citrus fruit that could be mistaken for a satsuma and then point to them one by one and say, "Not this, not this, not this, but THIS, this is a satsuma!" Wouldn't that clarify, remove confusion, and establish beyond doubt that this and only this is a satsuma? Some of the others may look kind of like a satsuma but they are not a satsuma.

When the thing we seek to know has obvious characteristics and stands out from everything else around it in appearance, it is easy to study it as it is. (Like the persimmon in a bowl with other assorted fruits.) But if the object of our study is something that is easily confounded with other things, (like the satsuma in a bowl with other citrus fruits), if it can be mistaken for other similar looking objects then the negation method of explaining something becomes a very useful tool.

Likewise, the Self is easily confused and mistaken for the 3 bodies, the 5 sheaths, the 3 states of experience. Therefore, we point to each and every one of the above things and say, "*neti, neti*- not this, not this.

As part of the definition of *Atma*, we see that it is not

part of the 3 states of experience (waking state, dream state and sleep state) but rather the observer of the 3 states. We need to contemplate further on this aspect to understand a few things better. The definition says that Consciousness or Self or *Atma* is the observer/witness of all 3 states. That means the *Atma* is the witness, the one who tells us that we are awake, that we are dreaming or that we are sleeping.

It is not difficult at all to see how we know we are awake; we simply say that our senses are alert and they tell us we are awake, so we know we are awake. In reality, it is Consciousness shining through our Gross body that makes us "know" we are awake.

In the dream state, all our senses are turned off, only our memory is active; actively playing back images and experiences from its inexhaustible stores. So how do we know we are dreaming? The waking state entity does not exist in the dream state, yet when we wake up, we know we were dreaming. Who or what tells us this? Again, when we dream, it is Consciousness/Self/*Atma* that shines inwards, illuminating the dream world for us. This Consciousness/Self/*Atma* tells us that we were dreaming.

When we are in deep sleep or dreamless sleep, we are in a state of total ignorance since all our organs, sensory and motor and even the internal instruments (4 aspects of the mind) are turned off. Because all these are non-functional, we are in complete ignorance, meaning we know nothing, as we have seen in the description of the deep sleep state (*pg. 154*).

When we say, "I know this", the "I" we mean here is almost always the Ego of the Subtle body that claims ownership of knowledge, any knowledge. And we have just explained that the Subtle body does not "exist" in the deep sleep state. Therefore, the true Ego or "I" as we know it, is also not functioning.

So, keeping in mind that we are talking about the Ego, the "I" that declares whether something is known or not, how can a person claim to have slept deeply since that "I" entity was not there to make such a declaration?

We have to infer that something else must have been there, observing the deep sleep, that tells us that we slept well. We have to note that whatever that is (which is telling us this fact) could not have slept, since it has borne witness to our deep sleep. It is also a requirement that the witness who has witnessed the deep sleep should also be present in the waking state to "give" witness, to testify. Therefore, it follows that it can be Consciousness alone that illuminated this deep sleep stage, which is also present in the waking state, telling us that we slept deeply.

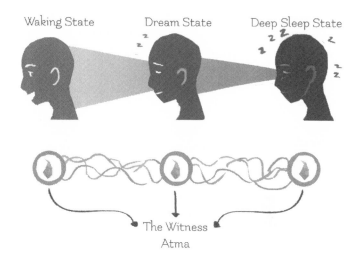

Figure 10. Atma is the witness of the 3 states

Another way to look at it is that a common entity that is present and is witness to the waking, dreaming, and sleeping states has to exist and we call that entity *Atma*/Self/Consciousness.

Part III

– 1 –

WHAT IS *ATMA*?

Let us recollect the definition of *Atma*. "The one who is distinct from the Gross, Subtle and Causal bodies, who is beyond the five levels (layers or sheaths) of experience, being the witness of the three states, that which remains in the form of existence, consciousness and fullness, that is the Self, *Atma*."

We are now entering into the heart of the matter- the discussion about *Atma*. In order to do this, let us start by learning about Consciousness and borrowed consciousness.

We have already examined in depth about the 3 bodies (*Sharira Trayam*), the Gross body, the Subtle body, and the Causal body. In their descriptions we have learned that they are made up of matter: gross matter, subtle matter, and even more subtle matter, respectively. But all 3 are made up of matter. Matter by its very nature is insentient, meaning it has no awareness. In other words, all matter is inert. According to *Vedanta*, inertness is defined as,

-that which has no consciousness
-that which cannot produce consciousness

We can take the above two principles and apply them to the 3 bodies and see if they are sentient or not. Our 3 bodies are material in nature and are therefore inert. They do not have consciousness, nor can they produce consciousness. So according to scripture the 3 bodies are inert, non-conscious and insentient in nature.

This means that not only is the Gross body inert, every part of the Subtle body is also inert. Even the mind (being part of the Subtle body) is inert matter and therefore insentient. Mind lacks consciousness of its own, nor can it produce consciousness.

It is the same with the Causal body. So, the 3 bodies lack sentiency.

All the above sounds logical, yet our direct experience seems to tell us something else. We feel our body to be conscious; conscious of itself and things around it. And our mind, it is far from being inert, it is conscious and very much sentient.

So logically the 3 bodies are known to be insentient, but experience tells us they are sentient. So how do we resolve this apparent contradiction?

Vedanta resolves this by giving the following example. Let us suppose we know of a poor man, a beggar who begs outside a temple every day. One day we see him as a guest at a wedding, dressed in fine clothes and expensive jewelry. We are taken aback to see him in all this finery. Yet we know him to be a destitute man. How do we understand this? We investigate a little and find out that he has borrowed the fine clothes and jewelry from someone else, which he is passing off as his own. Similarly, the 3 bodies, inert as they are, have borrowed their "consciousness" from somewhere else. Again, by logic if there is a borrower, there must also be a lender. So, who is the one who is lending consciousness to the 3 bodies? And to be a true lender, he should not be borrowing it from someone else. This lender of consciousness is *Atma/Self*.

Atma is the all-important 4th component (in addition to the 3 bodies). Without this, the 3 bodies will remain inert. Let us look at this concept with an example.

Let us think of a light bulb. When we say a light bulb, we have to think of the filament inside the bulb itself. We see it shine when we switch it on. Now what makes it shine is the electricity flowing through it. When it flows through the filament, it heats it up and the bulb shines. Although the main cause of the light is electricity, it is invisible to us. What we see with our eyes is the bulb, burning bright. Without electricity there will be no light. The bulb and its components are akin to our 3 bodies. The electricity that makes it glow is the *Atma* in our case. Just like the main power behind the light, the electricity is invisible, we cannot see, touch, or feel the *Atma*. However, just like we know that it is the electricity which makes the bulb glow, we have to know that it is the *Atma* that "blesses" the 3 bodies by lending them Consciousness, thereby making them appear sentient.

So, all our 3 bodies, including our much-valued mind, only appears to be conscious because they have borrowed consciousness from *Atma*.

– 2 –

THE SIX
CHARACTERISTICS
OF *ATMA*

Earlier we learned about *Atma* by the principle of negation. That is, we explained what *Atma* is not. This method helped us identify the usual things *Atma* get mistaken for. But saying what something is not, is not enough to know something. We also have to say what it is. In that context, we shall now study the characteristics of *Atma*.

1. *Atma* is the nature of Consciousness:

Atma is a non-material principle. What does this mean? This means that *Atma* is not made up of matter. As we saw earlier, matter cannot possess consciousness nor can it produce consciousness. The 3 bodies however are made up of matter. Being material in nature they are insentient and borrow consciousness from the *Atma*.

Atma being the original lender should not be borrowing consciousness from elsewhere. This means that *Atma* must be non-material in nature. It is of the nature of Consciousness itself.

2. *Atma* is an independent principle:

Atma is an independent principle because it is of the nature of Consciousness which is not dependent on matter for either its creation or existence. Previously we said matter can neither have nor produce consciousness. If matter possessed consciousness, then Consciousness would depend on matter. If matter is the source of or produced consciousness, then also Consciousness will depend on matter. Since Consciousness does not belong to matter and is not produced by matter, Consciousness is an independent principle which does not depend on matter either for its creation or existence.

3. *Atma* is attribute less:

Attributes mean properties that a certain thing possesses, qualities, traits, or characteristics. *Atma* is free from all qualities or traits. How is this possible?

Let us look at some examples of attributes. They can be small/large, soft/hard, loud/quiet, wet/dry, sweet/bitter to name a few. These are attributes as perceived by our 5 senses: eyes, ears, tongue, nose, and skin. These attributes arise from the nature of the raw materials they are made up of. For example, hot water from the tap is hot and liquid because being liquid is the nature of the Water element and it is hot because of the presence of the Fire element in the form of heat. The 5 elements (*panchamahabhutas*) are the basic building blocks of all matter in the known universe.

Since *Atma* is not made up of matter, we cannot look for qualities in it as one would for a material object.

Therefore, *Atma* is free of attributes.

4. *Atma* is eternal and beyond Time:

Atma does not depend on matter for its existence or creation. Even when matter disintegrates or perishes, *Atma* continues to survive; just as electricity continues to survive even if the light bulb is destroyed. We do not see light from a broken light bulb because the bulb is not functioning, not because electricity is no longer there. Non-manifestation of electricity does not mean non-existence of electricity.

So even when the physical body dies, *Atma* continues to exist. Therefore, *Atma* is eternal. Eternal is called *Nitya* in *Sanskrit* (*pg. 33* for *Nitya-Anitya viveka*).

Science points out that our universe is four dimensional; the first three are spatial dimensions, the fourth dimension is time. What that means is that everything that exists in the universe can be defined by these four variables. The location of the object is pinpointed by the x, y, and z variables. We use this to say where it is in 3-dimensional space. Let us take for example, a chandelier that is hanging in a room. We can describe its location by saying it is 4 feet from the entrance of the room, 8 feet from the southern wall and 7 feet from the floor. Now this chandelier was here yesterday, and it is here today. Although its location parameters have not changed, something has changed. And that is the time variable. The time yesterday can be denoted by t1 and the time today is denoted by t2 (t for Time).

We can describe the chandelier yesterday as 4x,8y,7z, t1, and the same chandelier today as 4x,8y,7z, t2. By this very description they are two different objects due to the change in the time variable.

"What could have changed in the chandelier within a span of a day that it needs two different descriptions?", we may ask.

Let us consider this. Suppose it is not the difference of one day but let us say 10 years pass. Will the chandelier be the same? If no one has moved it, its location would be the same. But with the passage of time, it would show dust, rust, and other evidence of wear and tear. So, the chandelier we see now will be different compared to the one we started out with 10 years ago. Why? Simply because of the passage of time. This is why time is also included in the complete description of something. But the change in a chandelier from one day to another is going to be so small that we ignore the significance of time, in this context. But in some cases like scientists in labs conducting experiments where observations are made from one millisecond to the next, time is a very important variable in the description of objects.

This was just to help us understand that time is a property of the material universe. And Consciousness being non-material, does not have the property of time. *Atma* is beyond time and is unconditioned by time.

5. *Atma* is all pervasive:

As we saw earlier, time and space are closely related. The 3 spatial dimensions along with the time dimension (often thought of as one word, Spacetime) can be used to describe most objects in the universe. Space is again a property of the material universe. But if something exists outside of the constructs of Spacetime, then we cannot describe or define it using the spatial dimensions, just as we could not use the time dimension to describe it.

Since *Atma* is not part of the material universe, it is beyond the confines of space. It is not restrained by, not conditioned by, and not circumscribed by space. It cannot have one pinpoint location. It is not located in the *Sharira Trayam* (3 bodies). It is behind (the power behind) the 3 bodies. In fact, it is behind all *Sharira Trayams*, small or big.

Just think about this: electricity is not only behind the small bulb but also the large bulb, the mid-sized bulb. In fact, it is behind all the individual bulbs in a string of light bulbs. It is there in between the bulbs too but we do not see the electricity in between because there is no bulb to light up and show us. Similarly, *Atma* is all pervasive and it is behind all the *Sharira Trayams*.

6. There is another 6ᵗʰ attribute of *Atma*.

Atma is non-dual. This is a little difficult to understand at this moment, but it will become clearer as we go on. But it takes off from the previous example of the electricity and the string of light bulbs. Electricity exists even in between light bulbs. Electricity is not something special for one light bulb and is something else for another light bulb. In fact, electricity is just one; a universal, non-dual entity. *Atma* is also like the electricity in the above example. It is one universal entity, lighting up different light bulbs.

– 3 –

THE PERSONAL CV

Now armed with all this knowledge let us go back to the original question of identity. As you must have seen by now, whenever we find a new piece of information, we study it and then fit in into the big question of identity.

Now, let us ask the question again, *"Who am I?"*

Vedanta says that the usual answers we give to this question (I am a doctor, I am a student etc.), are to be considered as our CV or resume for the outside world. But within ourselves, to ourselves when we ask that question, this is what we should say:

"Who am I?"

- I am the nature of Consciousness
- I do not depend on anything for my creation or my existence

- I am attribute-less
- I am eternal
- I am all pervasive
- I am non-dual

The most important lesson of *Vedanta* is to claim this *Atma* as our identity.

But how do we do this? How do we train ourselves to claim our own identity, for this internal transformation?

We do this by understanding the Seer-Seen discrimination exercise. Seer in this case is the one who sees and Seen is the object being viewed. We can also call this the Knower-Known discrimination. The Knower is the one who knows (by observation) and all the other things that he knows come under the Known. The exercise is to learn to identify ourselves as the Seer or the Knower of objects/events and that the objects/events are the Seen or the Known. They are seen or known by the Seer/Knower- us and are therefore different from us. This sounds very straightforward and easy, making us wonder what is so difficult about this exercise. The difficult part is learning to identify and distinguish between me-the Seer and not me- the Seen. We will go into greater detail on this subject in a few minutes.

By repeatedly employing this exercise in every aspect

of our lives, we can train ourselves to take possession of our true identity.

At the same time, we cannot be petty, disgruntled, bitter, or angry while making the claim, "I am eternal, all pervasive, limitless *Atma*."

They simply do not go together. Here is where the qualifications (*pg. 50*) and training of *karma yoga* and *upasana yoga* (*pg. 58*) come into play. If our mind is not adequately prepared by attaining the prerequisites, then we will run into the above phenomenon; of knowing we are *Atma* but behaving petty, disgruntled, bitter, and angry. *Jnana yoga* will ask us to claim that independent, eternal, all pervasive, non-dual *Atma* as our identity, but the unprepared mind will continue to identify with and carry the attributes of the mind-body-sense organ complex. And although our eyes may read this information on paper, we will be unable to internalize it and it will remain as words on a page. So, preparation is the key to a successful study. If we run into this, and as a beginner we will, we should go back and practice more *karma yoga* and *upasana yoga* depending on where we are stuck. Here is where a compassionate teacher is vital. He can guide us to the appropriate practice based on our individual struggle and help us imbibe the knowledge with confidence.

The answer to whatever struggle we may be caught up in will usually be more *karma yoga* or more *upasana yoga*. At this point it is important to clarify that this does not mean we have to renounce our body or practice austerities like the *yogis*. Definitely not!

What this just means is that we have to stop identifying with our body-mind-sense organ complex as our primary identity. We can still use our body to live and transact with the world like regular people. This is an internal transformation from one identity to another; outwardly we can go about our everyday business.

The Seer-Seen Discrimination methodology involves the application of the two fundamental laws of *Vedanta*.

Law 1: *I am different from whatever I witness/experience*

I am the observer; the witness and I am distinct from the objects I observe or witness. E.g.: I observe the sofa, I am not the sofa. Likewise, I experience this body, this mind, but I am not this body or this mind. I experience the *Sharira Trayam*, but I am not the *Sharira Trayam*.

I am always the observer and never the observed. This is part of the first law. Every time we see or experience something, we must keep this distinction in our mind. This brings about the detachment that is needed to embark on the path to true understanding. For example, when I meditate, I am not the meditator, I am the one observing the meditator (*pg. 63*).

Law 2: *I am free from all the attributes of the objects I witness/experience.*

All attributes (meaning qualities) belong to the world or the body or the mind. They define material objects. And these are in the realm of the "experienced" and hence they have attributes. But I, the observer of these attributes, the witness of these attributes, am free from all attributes.

This second law helps us to firmly keep sight of the fact that the passing attributes I see (like young/old, soft/hard, happy/sad) belong to the material world which I observe. I, being the observer, am free of all these qualities.

By constantly applying these 2 laws, we can work our way towards claiming *Atma* as our true identity.

Now, an astute student can ask, "Doesn't that mean that everything in the world is divided into two: one is the 'seer/observer', and all the rest is the 'seen/observed'? That means there are two things in the world:

meaning there is duality. *Advaita Vedanta* by definition is non-dual, so how can we say there are two things?"

This is a particularly important question which can be answered in many different ways.

But this is how I visualize it. I am now at the start of my *Advaita* education. Let us recollect the definition of *Advaita*. *Advaita* is the non-dualist approach to *Vedanta*. It does not accept that the human and the divine are two different entities. It declares that there is no dualism in anything we come across in the universe. Everything that exists, is only one.

Right now, in the uninitiated state, I am working under the premise that the world is an extremely complicated thing with innumerable events and people in it, working in unpredictable ways. Right now, my world has billions and billions of things, emotions, actions, people, and circumstances in it. As a first step, after all the preparation and *jnana yoga*, I have narrowed down that world from billions and billions to two things: the Seer and the Seen or the Knower and the Known. Now that in itself is a big improvement. The next step, the difficult (or some may say the easy) step is to realize that there are no two things but in fact only one.

If the word "witness" is taken for its most common meaning, then it follows that there is something else the witness "witnesses", thereby bringing about duality. Instead, think of the word witness to mean the entity, the sole entity that exists. For example, the Sun. The Sun is said to be a witness. He does not take a specific part in any of the activities that happen on Earth, yet without the Sun no activity can happen on Earth. So, although we say he is a witness, we should be saying he is more the cause, than the witness. Now, let us try again and view the word "witness" from the above angle. I am the witness of the world/body/mind. I exist (like the Sun) but without me, the world/body/mind cannot exist. Thus, we can go from billions to two and then from seemingly two to one (non-duality). We will see more of this, and it will become clearer.

- 4 -

ME AND NON-ME

We now take a closer look into the Seer-Seen or Knower-Known distinction. We need to be completely clear on this concept, so although this may seem somewhat repetitive, let us proceed. Looking at it from multiple angles helps consolidate the idea.

Where do we draw the line between me versus everything that is non-me? Usually, this line runs right around the perimeter of our body, of our skin. Everything inside that line is self and everything outside the line is non-self. So far things are clear. (Keep the definition and characteristics of *Atma* we have seen earlier, in your mind and follow along.)

Now, I have drawn this line and everything within it is me or self. Everything outside it including the room, the house, including you, your body, him, and his body are all non-self. Therefore, all things outside the line are non-me and are objects of my experience and therefore not me. I have included you and your body in my non-self. Similarly, when you draw your line you would have included me and my body and everything inside it as your non-self. As far as you are concerned, I am only an object of your experience and part of the "non-me" for you. If this line is really and truly the line of demarcation, then how can what is subject for me (myself/me) change into "non-self" and become an object when you draw your line? How can it be *Atma*? (this does not fit with the 6 attributes of *Atma*). So, this arbitrary line must be questioned.

From our discussions so far, what is the criteria for including the world as "not I"? Because it is known to me, known by me. Anything that is known by me cannot be me (Knower- Known discrimination).

The physical body by now, we are willing to accept is not me. If the line is not at the perimeter of our body, then where is it? Even all the experiences we undergo, we can accept to be not me. Maybe the line is at the level of our mind?

The hardest part to understand as non-me, is our mind. We possess a special kinship with our mind, our thoughts. And we often think of our mind as the Self. But in fact, just like the eyes or the ears, the mind is also an instrument, an instrument of knowledge.

Let us look at an example. We have a task. The task is that there is an apple and we have to see it. What happens when we attempt this? The eyes first see the apple. But then correspondingly, something happens in the mind. That which is happening in the mind when our senses give us a signal, is called a *vrtti*. The signal from the sense of sight has to create a matching change in the mind (which we call a *vrtti*) in order for the vision of the apple to appear. For every such cognition (sight- apple, book, table, or hearing- noise, bells, laughter, touch sensation- soft, rough etc.), a modification of the mind is required. Just like an image falls on our retina and casts its unique pattern, which is then erased and replaced by the next image we see, every cognitive signal casts a matching change in the mind only to be replaced by the next cognitive signal.

When our eyes move from the apple to a flower, our mind also now changes from the apple and then we see the flower. The mind changes and by the changes perceived, we know exactly what object is there in front of us (or rather in front of our eyes).

For every perception there is a change in the mind relevant to the object of perception. Now, that changed mind, is that seen by us or not? The answer is yes, it is. In fact, what we see all the time is what is happening in our mind, not what is happening outside, really. Whatever shape or form our mind assumes, that is the object we see. For example, many times a coiled rope or water hose is mistaken for a snake. What is there outside in reality is the rope or hose, yet our mind sees a snake and we jump back in fear. So, what do we really see? The object (rope) outside or the object (snake) inside? By some quirk, the rope the eyes saw, instead of creating the corresponding change for "rope" in the mind creates the change for "snake" and our mind sees a snake.

Although the eyes have seen the rope, the mind has seen the snake. And it is to what we see in the mind that we react. And whatever change that occurs in our mind in our thoughts, is what we are going to declare as what we saw. What do we learn from this? We learn that at all times whatever we come across is what is happening in our mind. We encounter the world only through the counter of the mind.

The mind undergoes a *vrtti*, a change, for say a table and we see a table. It undergoes a pot-*vrtti* for a pot, a car-*vrtti* for a car and so on. And we are the knower, the witness, of these *vrttis*. Now where shall we draw the line, the line between me and non me? Not at the mind.

– 5 –

Consciousness – *Cit*

L et us try again. Our quest for the unchanging *Atma*, can be viewed as the quest for the thing that is invariable amongst all the objects of cognition. Any object which we refer to as "this object" is an object of our knowledge. In other words, it is an object of our Consciousness. For example, the knowledge or cognition of a pot is pot-consciousness, which mean we are aware or conscious about what a pot is, what it looks like etc. Similarly, our knowledge of a car is car-consciousness, that of a tree is tree-consciousness and so on. From the point of view of the various senses, we have form-consciousness, sound-consciousness, touch-consciousness etc. Similarly, with reference to our body and its various layers (or *annamaya kosha, pranamaya kosha* etc.) we have body-consciousness, hunger consciousness, emotion consciousness, thought consciousness, memory consciousness etc. What is constant in all these? Consciousness, consciousness is constant.

This also extends to time-consciousness and space-consciousness. We are aware of space in terms of distance, and there we have space-consciousness. We become aware of time, past, present, and future and we have time-consciousness. When we become aware of our own ignorance of something, we have ignorance-consciousness. Both ignorance and knowledge are included as objects of consciousness. Our memory too. In all these, the one thing that is always present is consciousness. This Consciousness is the knower, the seer, the hearer, the I, the *Atma*.

Now the question is, "Is this Consciousness objectified by us?"

Let us do this simple exercise. Let me say a few words and as I say the word, see that object in your mind. Here we go.

Apple … tree … pen … Consciousness … rose … bicycle … bus … Consciousness … garden … table … Consciousness

Every time I said Consciousness, what did you see? Nothing. You did not see anything at all. Does that mean there is no Consciousness? No. All that it means is that when I say the word Consciousness, you did not see an object. This is because it is not an object.

Again, let us think of a goat, then think of a horse. In our mind the goat appears and then it is displaced by the horse. Now think of a cow. The horse is displaced by the cow. So, one object displaced the other. Now if we think of a tree, does it displace Consciousness? No. Think of the English language, does it displace consciousness? Think of the solar system, is Consciousness displaced? Remember something, recollect something, think of the past, think of the future, does it displace Consciousness?

What displaces Consciousness or "I"? If we think about it, the answer is nothing. Nothing can really displace Consciousness. I see a form, I (Consciousness) am there. I hear a sound, I am there. Any given emotion, I am there. Hunger, I am there. Recollection, cognition, I am there. I am there all the time.

What does not need to be objectified is "I". That is what Consciousness is. Everything is bathed in Consciousness.

Let us go further. Consciousness, I, alone is self-revealing, everything else depends on Consciousness to be revealed. There is an analogy used in the scripture, from the point of view of vision/ eyesight. To see an object the absolute essential requirement is light. Now, the object can be self-luminous or opaque. Stars like the sun are luminous, while planets and satellites like our moon are opaque and reflect light in order to be seen. In *Sanskrit* there are two words that describe this: *bhati*, that which shines first and *anubhati*, that which shines after. So, the sun is *bhati* and the moon is *anubhati*. Likewise, any opaque object, like this table in the room, cannot be seen in the dark. If we switch the room light on, then we can see the table. The light is *bhati* and the table shines after the light, hence the table is *anubhati*. The light lights up the table. The *Upanishads* take this imagery further and apply it to the process of cognition.

We just said that the sun is self-luminous and therefore *bhati*. Now can the self-luminous sun, *bhati* as it may be, be seen by me if my eyes are closed? No. So the sun is luminous only if my eyes are open when my eyes light up the sun. The eyes have to light up the moon, the planets and everything else be they self-luminous or opaque. So, everything shines after my eyes. Without the eyes, even light cannot reveal itself, so in this imagery, everything shines after the eyes. So, the eyes are *bhati*.

Can the eyes shine, *bhati*, without a mind? No. So the eyes now become *anubhati* because they shine after the mind, and the mind is *bhati*. So, after what does the mind shine? After "I" or Consciousness.

I shine all the time. I shine whether the mind shines or not. When the mind sleeps, I shine, so that on waking I can say, "*I slept well*". When the mind dreams, I shine and light up the dreams. When the mind is awake, the eyes are open, and I light up the eyes which in turn light up all the objects and forms. So, in every perception, form-perception, taste-perception, sound-perception, thought-perception, what is invariant and what lights up each one of them is the self-evident "I". I shine all the time. Even when Time and Space are distorted and folded up during dream and sleep, I shine. I am the Consciousness that lights up everything. This is what is called *Cit*.

Here and now we are ready to define, "What is *Atma*?" We have seen in the past, all the things it is not. Now we shall see what it is, rather what is its nature.

Atma is *Sat-Cit-Ananda svarupa*. (*svarupa* means of the nature of)

The nature of *Atma* is existence (*Sat*), consciousness (*Cit*) and fullness (*Ananda*).

In the previous paragraphs we derived clearly what is *Cit* (consciousness). We shall study *Sat* and *Ananda* next.

– 6 –

CONSCIOUSNESS – SAT, ANANDA

What is *Sat*? *Sat* is that which exists in all the 3 time periods. Here the 3 periods of time are past, present, and future. *Atma* is *Sat*; *Atma* exists in the past, present and future. What we are now going to delve into is the concept of time. This may seem a bit confusing but with some patience it does become clear.

As an exercise, think of the past, maybe your last birthday, an event in the past. When you think of this past event, do you think of it in the present or in the past? In the present, of course. When you think of the events of the year 1986, or last Valentine's day, you think of them in the present. We always think of the past in the present.

Now let us think of the future. Think of a year from now. Where do you think about the future? Now or in the future? Now. So, the future is also now, the past is also now. Strange is it not? We can dwell all we want in the past or dream all we want about the future. Both events happen in the "now". This is another reason why the emphasis is always on "live in the moment, live in the present", there really is nowhere else to live!

Since the "now" is the very embodiment of time, if we want to know about time, we need to learn about the "now". Usually our concept of now implies time, a length of time. When we are aware of a length of time, we have time consciousness (*pg. 187* on object consciousness). When we want to think of a particular length of time in the present, we can think of the present decade, the present year, the present month, present week, or present day. Can we agree that the present day, today, is the "present"? What if we do not want to stop there, we can go on to the present hour, the present minute, the present second. Then can we agree the present second is the "present"? What if we do not want to accept that and go even further and say, a second has microseconds and therefore the present microsecond should be the present. Again, why stop there? So mathematically we can dissect and never quite decide what is the present.

But whichever length of time we end up choosing as our present, we have to agree that there is Consciousness,

consciousness of that length of time. If we keep looking into it further, (seconds to microseconds and so forth), time itself is erased and what remains is only Consciousness. Consciousness does not come or go. It simply *is there*.

Time consciousness is now-consciousness. In this now-consciousness what is the length of this "now"? As we just saw, there is no certain or definite length of time for this "now". There is no length of time. This is what is called *Sat*. It is not what is bound by time, but it is the truth of time. This existence across time, whatever length of time we have chosen, is what is *Sat*.

Atma is *Cit* and *Sat*. We now have to understand the third quality, *Ananda*. *Ananda* is of the form of happiness. It is fullness or wholeness. What is this connection between wholeness and happiness?

Whenever there is a moment of happiness, it is due to the temporary removal of distance between the seeker and the sought. Think back to an instance when you were happy. When you got that job you wanted or that person you yearned for, the distance between you and what you wanted was removed and you felt whole. It is this feeling of wholeness that gave you happiness. In fact, we do not need that external thing (job, person etc.) to "make" us whole. We only have to realize that we are whole and full in ourselves.

The true me or I, is *Atma*, which is *Ananda* (wholeness). This is why *Ananda* can also be translated as bliss.

From the above explanations, we can see why each and every one of us is *Sat-Cit-Ananda svarupa*.

I hope by now, we have a clear understanding of who we are and who or what we are not. To review, I am not my Gross, Subtle or Causal body. I am the witness of all the things that happen to me. I am the subject and the only subject of every object and that "I" am *Atma* whose very nature is Consciousness, unlimited by time and always whole.

This *Atma*, the real I, is covered by different layers (the 5 *koshas*), encased in the 3 bodies and through these casings, I observe and experience the 3 states (waking, dream, and sleep). Even though I now know I am all-pervading *Atma*, I still have to acknowledge the Causal, Subtle and Gross body.

We have to grasp that this whole set up is an intelligent arrangement of things, put together so that we can experience the world.

The previous chapters have explained in detail how we are put together. They have also explained that "I" am limitless and whole, so now the question arises, how about other things in the world? How are those created? In fact, how is the whole universe created? And what is my relationship to those objects if I am the whole?

- 7 -

CREATION

One of the most important sayings in *Vedanta* is "*Tat Tvam Asi*". This is one of the *mahavakyas* (*maha* means great and *vakya* mean saying or words).

Translated, *Tat Tvam Asi* means "You are That". At first glance the translation really has not helped at all. In fact, it makes no sense. We can follow up until "You are", it's the "That" that throws us. We have understood in great detail who we are, so we know the meaning of the "You are" part. Now what is this, "That"? In other words, we have learned about Tvam *Asi* (You are), now have to search for the meaning of *Tat* (That).

So far, we have studied and understood "Who am I?". This exercise is akin to the study of the microcosm. Now, we move on to the study of the macrocosm. Here we are entering into the world of cosmology according to the *Vedas*. We will try to understand Creation according to

Vedanta, in order to explain the "That", which is all that we see around us. The saying is, You are That. It means "You are all that you see around you".

This statement is an equation. An equation has some expression on the left-hand side and some expression on the right-hand side and these are linked by the "=" sign, to indicate that the items on both sides of the sign are equal.

You = all that is around you.

We already know the left-hand side of the equation.

We need to study the right-hand side of the equation. To understand "All that is around you" we have to look at Creation. Only then can we get a clear picture of all that is around us. After knowing that, we can compare the two sides of the equation and decide if they are equal or not.

In fact, "Creation" is not the right word. A better word would be manifestation. As we all know from the Law of Conservation of energy and matter, nothing can be created or destroyed, but merely converted from one form to another. So, how can the universe alone be "created"? We have to reword it as: when the previously unmanifest, dormant form of the universe is manifested, we call it Creation. By extension, the universe cannot be destroyed. Instead when it retreats into its unmanifest, dormant form, we call this Destruction. But for the sake of convenience, we can call this manifestation, Creation. Having cleared this basic confusion, we can now proceed.

What do we mean by manifest and unmanifest? Manifest is what is available for transaction (by our sense organs and internal instruments). Unmanifest is that which is not available for transaction, but it exists, nonetheless.

Let us look at an example. Think of milk, it is manifest as milk, we can drink it or spill it or do whatever we want with it. Now think of butter. We know that it is present (in its rudimentary form) in the milk, but is it available for us to transact with? Can we see the butter with our eyes, taste it on our tongue? We can only see and taste the milk but not the butter. It is unmanifest. Only when it undergoes a transformation (by churning and other processes) the butter "comes into existence" or as we may say, butter is "created". But in fact, all that has happened is that it has changed from unmanifest form to manifest form. But even though we cannot see or taste the butter in the milk, through knowledge (which is *jnana yoga* in our case) we know that the butter is there in the milk. Since we already possess this knowledge, it seems amazingly easy and straightforward. Now imagine how it looks to a child or to someone who does not have this knowledge and is coming across this for the first time. To him it would look miraculous!

Now let us take this and apply it to Creation and then we begin to understand.

Before the creation of the transactable universe, the universe existed in a potential, unmanifest form. This form is undifferentiated, meaning it does not have galaxies, starts, planets and other celestial bodies in it. It is in the form of pure, invisible undifferentiated energy. We call this Causal matter. This could be small particles, sub particles of atoms, or mere energy particles. It is as yet unseen, unsee able, not because of their size alone, but because it is so subtle that it cannot be perceived by any of our sensory organs. This Causal matter is called *Maya*. This Causal matter also includes our Causal Body (or *Karana Sharira* we saw under the 3 bodies we possess).

But wait, we have to take into consideration that one more thing that must have existed before creation. In the previous chapters, we saw that *Atma* is the Consciousness principle. It is non-material in nature and therefore does not come within time and space. We also conceded that Consciousness is beyond time and space which means Consciousness has to be eternal. This means that before the Creation, Consciousness should have also existed.

Now we have two things that existed before Creation

(again let us remember this word is used just for convenience). What are these two things?

1. *Atma* or Consciousness, unconditioned by, un-influenced by, un-circumscribed by the time-space principle
2. The whole material of Creation in unmanifest form as Causal matter called *Maya*

So *Atma* and *Maya* existed. This Consciousness at the level of an individual is called *Atma* and at the level of the cosmos is called *Brahman*. This is why these two terms were used interchangeably in the earlier part of our discussion. (*pg. 72*, it would not have made much sense to explain this then.) So *Atma* equals *Brahman*. They are both the same thing. Then why do we have two names? *Atma* is used to refer to Consciousness at the level of the individual or the microcosm and *Brahman* is used to refer to Consciousness at the level of the macrocosm.

Now let us look at some of the differences between *Maya* and *Brahman*.

– 8 –

BRAHMAN AND MAYA

There is one similarity between *Brahman* and *Maya*. And that is, both existed before Creation. The differences are more important.

1. *Brahman* is the non-material principle, whereas *Maya* is the material principle. As explained earlier, material principle means that which exists within Spacetime and is made up of the 5 great elements. And non-material principle is that with is outside of Spacetime and is not material in nature.

2. *Brahman* has no properties since it is non-material in nature. *Maya* on the other hand, being matter, has many different properties.

3. *Brahman* is indivisible, it is one undivided Consciousness. *Maya*, which is matter, is highly

divisible, it multiplies and can take many shapes and forms.

4. *Brahman* is changeless. It does not have attributes to start with, and therefore does not change. *Maya* is matter, it cannot stay still and one of its main qualities is change.

So, these two entities start the process of Creation. *Brahman* along with *Maya* is given the name *Isvara*. Here before we go into actual Creation, we need to clear up a few things. From the way I have laid it out so far, it looks like two things (*Brahman* and *Maya*) created the universe. Isn't that duality? Two things? Actually no. There is only one thing, that is *Brahman*. The second thing, *Maya*, is the power of *Brahman* to create. For the sake of explaining the set up and the processes of Creation, we have split them up into two things.

Let us look at an example to clarify what we mean. Think of a gold chain.

There is the metal, gold and there is the chain made of gold. The truth of the chain is gold. The chain has no existence without gold. Gold is gold and the chain is also gold. If we remove the gold, the chain ceases to exist. There is no chain. If we remove the chain, gold does not cease to exist. It may be left behind as a molten blob or some other shape of gold. Likewise, the truth of existence is *Brahman*, like the gold and *Maya* is like the chain.

Let us think about a scenario where we want to create something, a creative process. The creative process requires two things.

1. There has to be a creator, who possesses the knowledge and skills to create. He is referred to as the efficient cause. The creator is the efficient cause.
2. And in order to make his creation, he needs material, something with which to make the creation out of. That second thing is called the material cause.

An artist creates a painting and his materials are canvas, paint, brushes etc. Similarly, when the creator is a sculptor, his creation is a statue and his materials are the stone and chisels etc.

In the above examples, the creator and his materials are two separate things.

But my favorite example is that of the spider. Think of a spider spinning a web. The spider is the creator, the web is its creation. But what does it make the web with? What is its raw material and what are its tools? In the case of the spider, the spider itself is the raw material and the tools. The spider makes the web from its own secretions and fashions the web not with outside tools but using itself as the tool.

So, in the case of the spider, it is the creator and it is also the material of its creation.

Now we can see how it is possible to refer to *Brahman* as the creator and also say *Brahman* is the material cause of the creation. This material cause is what we had referred to earlier as *Maya* or Causal matter.

This discussion is very reminiscent of a previous one (*pg. 87*): the discussion about *Satya* and *Mithya*. *Mithya* is anything that has borrowed its consciousness from something else. A *mithya* object has no independent existence of its own, it depends on another for its existence. And the thing that lends existence to the *mithya* object is what is called *satya*. So always, *satya* is real. *Mithya* does not mean nonexistent. Mithya means apparently real. (Discussed at length on *pg. 87*)

Maya is *mithya* and *Brahman* is *satya*.

Think again of the spider, the material with which it creates the web is itself. Likewise, *Brahman* is the efficient cause as well as the material cause. Like in the case of the spider web or the gold chain, without the efficient cause, namely the spider or the gold, the web and chain cannot exist. The spider and the gold can exist without the web and the chain respectively, but not the other way around. Similarly, *Brahman* can exist without *Maya*, but *Maya* cannot exist without *Brahman*. *Maya* is not a stand-alone, separate thing.

Brahman is *Brahman*, *Brahman* plus *Maya* is also *Brahman*. Think again of the spider. Spider by itself is also spider, spider plus the juice it makes (to ultimately make the web) is also spider. Juice does not stand by itself. This is beautifully summed up by the following statement, "There is only one thing, that is *Brahman*. The second thing, *Maya*, is the power of the *Brahman* to create."

At every step of our journey we have to remind ourselves that duality doesn't exist. Non-duality is the very basis of *Advaita Vedanta*. Whenever we come across what appears to be a duality, we must inquire into it and understand that the duality we see is only an apparent duality, used for the sake of explanation.

So now we are standing at the edge of Creation (or more accurately, manifestation) with a non-dual *Brahman* that is existing as the non-material *Brahman* and its creative power in the form of material *Maya*.

The term for this combined entity, *Brahman* plus *Maya* is *Isvara*. This is what is understood as God in general parlance.

– 9 –

THE TWO STAGES OF CREATION

Creation happens in two stages. We have to envision it as a seed becoming a tree. The first stage is the seed becoming a plant, the second stage is the plant becoming the fully grown tree. Creation and its two stages have to be understood at the level of the macrocosm (the universe) and the microcosm (the individual).

Maya, in the macrocosm, is made up of Causal matter (matter that is the cause of all further matter yet to be created). If we think back, the corresponding matter in the microcosm (that is us, the *Jivas*) is the *Karana Sharira* (which is why that was referred to as the Causal body).

This Causal matter as part of the first stage transforms into Subtle matter and the Subtle universe comes into being. It is not yet visible. The energy of the Causal matter is "condensed" into Subtle matter, made up of the 5 subtle elements. The corresponding matter in the microcosm is the Subtle body (*Sukshma Sharira*), which arises from the Causal body (*Karana Sharira*).

This is the first stage, Causal matter becoming Subtle matter. The 5 *Mahabhutas* are in their Subtle form; they are not available for transaction. The 5 elements and the order in which they come into being are:

First, Space or *Akasha,* then Air or *Vayu*, then Fire or *Agni*, then Water or *Jala* and finally Earth or *Prithvi*.

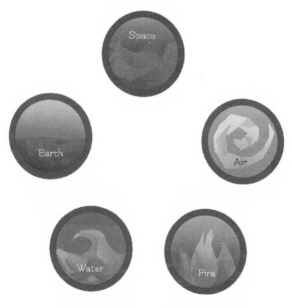

Figure 11. The 5 Mahabhutas (Elements)

We have to take note that "Earth" does not mean Earth alone, it refers to all solid forms of matter. Similarly, Water is all liquid matter etc.

Since the Subtle universe evolves from the Causal matter or *Maya*, it will have the attributes of *Maya*. So all the features present in *Maya* will be manifested in the universe and whatever attributes seen in the universe will also be seen in *Maya*.

The Scriptures elaborate that there are 3 types of energies in the universe.

1. Power of Knowledge or *Jnana Shakthi*
2. Power of Action or *Kriya Shakthi*
3. Inertia or *Dravya Shakthi*

In *Vedanta*, these 3 qualities are called *gunas*. All material things will possess qualities such as color, form, texture etc. These specific attributes are what help us distinguish them from one another. As Creation evolves, more and more complex matter comes into existence. The complexity comes about due to the comingling of different attributes. These attributes in their most primitive form are the *gunas*. And their interplay ensures the diversity we see. Now let us get an understanding of these 3 *gunas*.

1. *Sattva guna* or Power of knowledge. This is the ability to know things, to understand and to learn. It is written as *Sattvaguna*.
2. *Rajas guna* or Power of action. This is the power to act, to move and to bring about effect. This is used in a sentence as *Rajoguna*.
3. *Tamas guna* or Inertia. Inertia is absence of the knowing faculty and absence of the acting faculty. It cannot know neither can it act. This is referred to as *Tamoguna*.

These 3 *gunas* are present in *Maya* which is the material source of the entire universe.

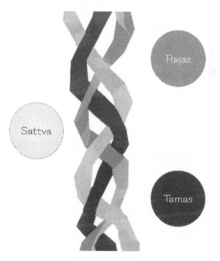

Figure 12. The 3 Gunas (Qualities)

The Subtle universe (which is the first to emerge from *Maya*) and the 5 subtle elements that make up the Subtle universe, also have these 3 *gunas*.

E.g. The subtle Earth element has *Sattva*, *Rajas* and *Tamas gunas*, the subtle Water element also has *Sattva*, *Rajas* and *Tamas gunas* and so on.

We have now completed a brief look at the first stage of Creation at the level of the macrocosm.

We shall now see how the first stage of Creation unfolds at the level of the microcosm.

As discussed earlier, each of the 5 subtle elements has 3 *gunas* (*Sattva*, *Rajas* and *Tamas*). This gives us 15 parts within the 5 subtle elements (3 multiplied by 5) to work with. From these 15 parts, all the components of the Subtle body (*Sukshma Sharira*) in the microcosm have to be formed. There is a very beautiful and orderly way in which this happens.

Let us recollect the components of the Subtle body (*pg. 104*):

5 sense organs
5 motor organs
5 *pranas*
4 internal instruments

Let us see how these are formed.

The 5 sense organs are our instruments of knowledge. So, it stands to reason that they should arise from the knowing faculty of the 3 *gunas*, which is the *Sattvaguna*. The 5 sense organs and their source of origin are as follows.

1. Organ of hearing (ear): From the *Sattva* aspect of Subtle Space element comes the sense organ of hearing.

2. Organ of touch (skin): From the *Sattva* aspect of Subtle Air element, comes the sense organ of touch.

3. Organ of sight (eye): From the *Sattva* aspect of Subtle Fire element comes the sense organ of sight.

4. Organ of taste (tongue): From the *Sattva* aspect of Subtle Water, comes the sense organ of taste.

5. Organ of smell (nose): From the *Sattva* aspect of Subtle Earth, comes the sense organ of smell.

Figure 13. Formation of the 5 Jnanendriyas
(Organs of Knowledge)

As we can see, all the sense organs are formed from the *Sattva* aspects of the 5 elements. As mentioned earlier, there is a method to this because *Sattvaguna* is the power of knowledge (*Jnana shakti*). The sense organs are the portals through which we "know" the world around us. (Here, we have to keep in mind that when we say sense organs, we are referring to the Subtle body.)

When the *Sattvaguna* of all the 5 Subtle elements

combine together, the 4 internal instruments (namely *Manas, Chitta, Buddhi and Ahamkara*) are born.

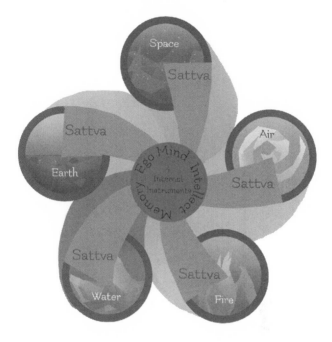

Figure 14. Formation of the 4 Antakaranas (Internal instruments)

When we learn about a particular object, say pizza, we engage our senses. We see the pizza, we smell the pizza, we reach out and touch the pizza and finally we taste the pizza. All that sensory information (collected from the subtle sense organs) goes into the mind for processing. The sense organs we know are derived from the *Sattvaguna* of the 5 elements. In order to process this information, the mind has to be derived from the *Sattva* aspect of all 5 of these sources. Again, we cannot help but marvel at the beauty of this arrangement.

Now on to the 5 motor organs. They are our organs of action. All the subtle motor organs are derived from the *Rajas aspect* of the 5 elements. *Rajoguna* is responsible for all action or activity. It is *kriya shakthi*, the power to move and create, therefore it makes sense that the *Rajas* aspect of the 5 great elements gives rise to all motor organs.

1. Organ of speech: From the *Rajas* aspect of Subtle Space element, the organ of speech is born

2. Organ of action (hands or grasping): From the *Rajas* aspect of Subtle Air element, the organ of action, hand is born.

3. Organ of movement (feet): From the *Rajas* aspect of Subtle Fire element, the organ of movement, feet, is born.

4. Organ of evacuation: From the *Rajas* aspect of Subtle Water element, the organ of evacuation/excretion is born.

5. Organ of reproduction: From the *Rajas* aspect of

Subtle Earth element, the organ of procreation is born

Figure 15. Formation of the 5 Karmendriyas (Organs of Action)

From the combined *Rajas* aspects of the 5 elements, the 5 *pranas* arise. These are the *Prana, Udana, Vyana, Samana* and *Apana*. These 5 *pranas* are what keep the body functioning. These *pranas* function and move within the body (in keeping with their *Rajasic* source) but they cannot perceive. Only sense organs and the internal instruments of the mind, which are from the *Sattva* source, can perceive.

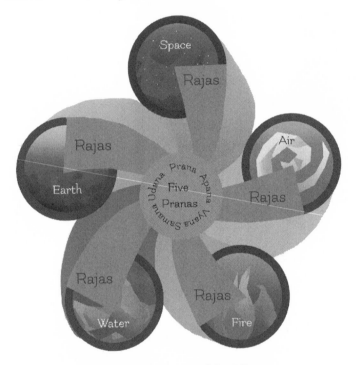

Figure 16. Formation of the 5 Pranas

Thus, all the 19 aspects of the Subtle body have formed.

The second stage of Creation is Subtle matter becoming Gross matter. Only at the Gross matter stage does a visible/transactable universe come into being.

This transformation occurs in both the macrocosm and microcosm.

Gross matter in the microcosm, as you would have guessed by now, is the Gross body or *Sthula sharira*.

How does this grossification take place?

Up until now, each of the 5 subtle elements are pure, meaning Subtle Air element has only air, Subtle Fire element is made up of only Fire and so on.

Now to create the next stage, we have to work with whatever is left over from the previous stage. The *Tamoguna* of all 5 Subtle elements are what are left over. During the final stage, the *Tamoguna* of all the 5 elements get mixed in various proportions to form the 5 gross elements.

So, each gross element is not pure, but is a mixture of all 5 elements. The gross Earth element has got not just the Earth element in it, but Space, Air, Fire and Water element also. In that case how do we distinguish each of the 5 gross elements if all of them are a mixture of the 5? We go about this by identifying the predominant element in the mixture because each Gross element is made by mixing the *Tamogunas* of the Subtle elements in a certain ratio.

For example, Gross Space is 50% Subtle space, the other 50% is made up of the other 4 remaining Subtle elements equally (12.5% Subtle Air, 12.5% Subtle Fire, 12.5% Subtle Water and 12.5% Subtle Earth)

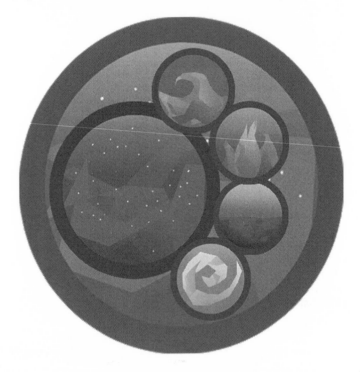

Figure 17a. Formation of Gross element Space

Gross Air element is made up of 50% Subtle Air element and the other 50% is made up of the 4 remaining Subtle elements equally (12.5% Subtle Space, 12.5% Subtle Fire, 12.5% Subtle Water and 12.5% Subtle Earth)

Figure 17b. Formation of Gross element Air

Gross Fire element is made up of 50% Subtle Fire element and the other 50% is made up of the 4 remaining Subtle elements equally (12.5% Subtle Space, 12.5% Subtle Air, 12.5% Subtle Water and 12.5% Subtle Earth)

Image 17c. Formation of Gross element Fire

Gross Water element is made up of 50% Subtle Water element and the other 50% is made up of the 4 remaining Subtle elements equally (12.5% Subtle Space, 12.5% Subtle Air, 12.5% Subtle Fire and 12.5% Subtle Earth)

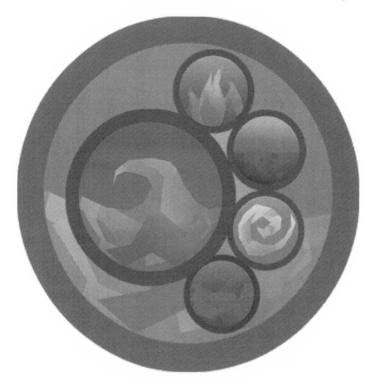

Image 17d. Formation of Gross element Water

Gross Earth element is made up of 50% Subtle Earth element and the other 50% is made up of the 4 remaining Subtle elements equally (12.5% Subtle Space, 12.5% Subtle Air, 12.5% Subtle Fire and 12.5% Subtle Water)

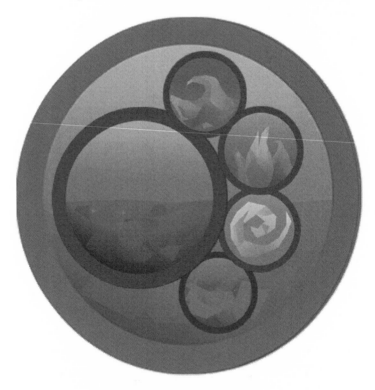

Figure 17e. Formation of Gross element Earth

Upon creation of the Gross elements, the entire Cosmos comes into existence. By various permutations and combinations these 5 Gross elements create the infinite variety of things in the universe, including our own physical bodies, those of animals, plants and inanimate objects like mountains, oceans and even stars: all are combinations of the same 5 Gross elements. This is *Vedic* Cosmology in a nutshell.

– 10 –

MAKING SENSE OF *ADVAITA*

After gathering all the information above, let us try to organize our knowledge by understanding it in relation to the microcosm and macrocosm.

Principle	Macrocosm	Microcosm
Self	Brahman	Atma
Self (another name)	Paramatma	Jivatma
Causal	Causal matter	Karana Sharira
Subtle	Subtle matter	Sukshma Sharira
Gross	Gross matter	Sthula Sharira
Anatma (material principle)	Maya	Upadhis (5 sheaths, 3 bodies)
Self + Material principle	Brahman + Maya	Atma + Upadhis
Name given to Self + Material principle	Ishvara	Jiva

Principle	Macrocosm	Microcosm
Sattva	Revealing power	Mode of Awareness. Knowledge
Rajas	Projecting power	Mode of Passion, doing, "I want…"
Tamas	Veiling power, Matter, insentient, inert	Mode of Inaction, cannot act, cannot learn, "I feel…"

Table 4. Relationship between the macrocosm and the microcosm

From the above table we can see a pattern. The same thing exists at the level of the macrocosm (universe) and at the level of the microcosm (individual). The point to understand is that what exists at the two levels are not two separate entities instead they are merely two names for the same entity when it appears at the two levels.

Let us review what we have discovered so far. There is only one thing, one Consciousness, which is *Brahman* which acts through the material principle. When that Consciousness is functioning in an individual along with the 3 bodies (*Sharira trayam*), it is called a *Jiva*. When that same Consciousness functions in the entire Universe, along with Maya, it is called *Ishvara*. The *Atma* that lives in a *Jiva* can also be called *Jivatma*. The *Atma/Brahman* that lives in *Ishvara* can also be called *Paramatma*.

So, it is the one and the same *Atma* (*Brahman*) which is called *Jivatma* and *Paramatma* based on the medium through which it functions. Remove the medium, be it *Maya* or the *upadhis* which are inert, there is no *Jivatma* or *Paramatma*; only *Atma*. In the end, it is one *Atma* functioning through a material medium (which is also called *Anatma, an* means non, so *anatma means non-Atma*) under two names, *Jivatma* and *Paramatma*. And I am that *Atma*, I am that *Brahman*.

This is the "*Tat*" portion of the great saying *Tat Tvam Asi*, we came across earlier (*pg. 196*). This *Atma*, this *Brahman* who we have examined in great depth in the last few pages is *Tat*. The saying is "You are that". The "that" is *Brahman*. And as we have seen, *Brahman* is everything there is. There is nothing in the universe other than *Brahman*.

The inner meaning of the great saying can now be seen to be,

Everything is *Brahman* and you are that *Brahman*.

When I work behind this individual body, I am *Jivatma* and when I work behind the universe, I am *Paramatma*. This is how the apparent duality of there being a *Jivatma* and a *Paramatma* is negated. This is a fundamental teaching of *Advaita Vedanta*.

So far, we have delved deep and understood the relationship between *Jivatma* and *Paramatma*.

Now let us see the relationship between *Atma* (Consciousness) and *Anatma* (Matter). The relationship between these two is that of supporter- supported. What this means is that Matter is supported by Consciousness or Matter depends on Consciousness. Matter depends on Consciousness to even prove its existence. For example, how do we know an object exists? We have to either see it, hear it, touch it etc. (direct perception through our sense organs) or know about it (through the internal instruments of our mind). Both these are nothing but tools of Consciousness. So, to see a car or a clock or an atom, or electrons moving through double slits, there needs to be Consciousness.

On the other hand, what proof do we need to know we exist? Do we get up every morning and touch, see, hear ourselves before believing we exist? We just know we exist. We do not consult a meter or a measurement to know that. *"My existence is self-evident."* That is why Consciousness is *Satya* and all matter is *Mithya*. *Satya* is independent and *Mithya* is dependent. *Satya* is one whereas *Mithya* can be many. Hence there is only one Consciousness while there are many, many forms of matter in various shapes and sizes.

This is the central core of knowledge contained all the texts of *Advaita Vedanta*.

- *Brahman/Atma* or Consciousness is *Satya*
- Everything else, all matter, is *Mithya*
- *Jivatma* and *Paramatma* are one and the same *Brahman*

This in short, is the essence of Self-Knowledge. This is who we are. Each and every one of us is the ever whole, never divided, unbound by Time, eternal and eternally blissful in wholeness, *Brahman*.

How do we gain this knowledge? We gain this knowledge through *Jnana yoga* by going through the 3 stages (*pg. 80*).

- *Shravanam* – listening
- *Mananam* – reflecting
- *Nidhidyasanam* – practicing

During *Shravanam* only listening to the new knowledge takes place. When you simply read these pages for the first time it is *Shravanam*. Then you will question the way things have been described, you will search for other sources, compare them, and clear your doubts. This is

Mananam. And finally, after you are convinced, you will assimilate the new knowledge and start applying it in your everyday life. That is *Nidhidyasanam*.

Now after successful assimilation of this knowledge what happens? There are some things that happen while the individual is still alive and some other things that happen after death.

A person who has attained Self-Knowledge in this birth is called a *Jivan Muktha* (one who is free or Liberated while still living).

He is called a realized soul. He has realized. What has he realized? He has realized who he is.

And this realization has Liberated him.

Liberated him from what? Liberated him from the emotional and mental ups and downs of everyday life. All the problems of insecurity, fear, jealousy, anger, competition, desire etc. belong to the cycle of *samsara*. Since he has realized that he is beyond Time and Space and is the embodiment of eternally whole bliss, he has broken the cycle of *samsara*.

He is alive so he will have to undergo the events of life that he has still left to live. But all the unhealthy, distressing responses to life events as they happen to him are gone. To him, it is like watching a movie. All of us enjoy a movie every now and then. But never at any point do we take it to be real and grieve for the deaths in the movie nor do we wholly believe and revel in the happiness of the movie's happy ending. But we can watch and enjoy the movie, nonetheless. In order to enjoy the movie, completely believing and entering into the movie is not a requirement. One can just watch and then get up and leave. That is how life is transformed for a *Jivan Muktha*.

This makes him a person whose balance of mind is never disturbed. It also makes him a very independent person. He does not need things or people or constant adulation to be happy. He is independent of all that.

Next, what happens to him after death? For that we need to understand what happens to a non *Jivan Muktha* after death. In *Vedic* culture, we never say a person is dead, we always say he is gone. This is a reference to the fact that he has gone on a journey, a trip. So, for us, after death there is travel. Where do we travel to? Upon death, our Gross body lies lifeless on this earth. This Gross body is either buried or cremated. Either way it disintegrates and is broken down in to the 5 great elements. Each aspect is returned to the respective element. For example, when the body is buried, the water element in it is released as it putrefies and is absorbed by the soil to join other water sources, the bones go on to become part of the earth element and so on.

The Subtle and Causal bodies depart and go on this journey we referred to. They travel and then acquire another Gross body (based on their *karmas*- see next chapter). They live out another life span in that Gross body, experience *samsara* and die and travel again. This is the cycle of birth and death. This keeps on repeating. The life we are living currently is just one in a long series of such lives.

Now in the case of the *Jivan Muktha*, there is no rebirth in another Gross body. Since he has realized he is the same as *Paramatma* or *Brahman*, when he dies, he merges with the whole and there is no Subtle or Causal body left for rebirth. He has broken the so-called neverending cycle of birth and death.

Jnanam or Knowledge breaks the cycle by destroying all *karma*. And the person who has attained this knowledge is called a *jnani*. As we saw earlier (*pg. 101*) *karma* is the currency of transaction in this birth and beyond. No more currency means no more transactions.

- 11 -

KARMA AND THE JIVAN MUKTHA

We shall now talk about *Karma*. This is a much-mangled word, both in the Eastern and Western cultures. We have seen what *karma* truly means earlier (*pg. 52*) We will go into it in greater depth now.

Wherever there is "doer ship" there is *karma*. When we engage in action, we have to face the *karma* that that action generates. Whenever we perform an action, two types of results are generated: the seen and the unseen. As the name indicates, the seen set of results are what are visible to us. For example, we donate food and clothing to a charity. The benefits that result from this action when these objects get distributed are the visible results. We can see the effects in the here and now. It also produces in us a sense of happiness for having done some good for our community. Now simultaneously, this action also produces an invisible result. This invisible outcome is also *karma*. If the actions are good, it generates good *karma* (*punya*) or if the actions are bad, it will generate bad *karma* (*paapam*). The *punya* and *paapa* of every action we do accumulates in our individual account. And so, the account, the *karma* account, builds for every *Jiva* who is a doer.

Here a valid question arises. Won't the visible and invisible effects be the same? That is, if we give to charity, the visible result is the happiness and the contentment of helping others and the invisible result (*karma*) is also a positive one (*punyam*). So why have two types of results, visible and invisible? Let us imagine for a moment that we have given a large sum of money to charity, just to gain a good name and for it to look good on our resume. In this case the visible result may be good and positive, we have helped our community after all, irrespective of our intentions. But the invisible result (*karma*) of this action will not be all *punyam*, our selfish motives will taint that action with some measure of *paapam* too. The *karma* of our actions may be invisible, but the account is very real, and it forms the currency for all our transactions.

All of us are subjected to 3 kinds of *karma* in relation to time.

The new actions we do in this birth, in this birth as a human, is called *Agami karma*. Everything we do every day from the time we wake up to the time we go to bed, contributes towards the *Agami karma*.

The second kind of *karma* is called *Sanchita karma*. This is the accumulated *karma* from all our previous births. *Karma* once it is generated has to fructify before it is realized. So, the action I do today, stays in an account. It can stay in that account for any amount of time depending on the action and the other factors in play in the field at the time. The *karma* comes to fruit maybe the very next day or maybe after years, in this birth or many births later. *Sanchita karma* is accumulated *karma* that is waiting in my account over many births to fructify. The *Agami karma* that I am generating day to day goes into my *Sanchita karma* account to await fruition.

The third kind of *karma* is *Prarabdha karma*. This is the *karma* that has fructified and is bearing fruits as we speak. This *Prarabdha karma* is what is bringing about our day to day results. This birth, in this body, to these parents, this education, everything is *Prarabdha* manifesting. When the *Prarabdha karma* is exhausted the lifetime of the *jiva* is done. But is *karma* done? No. The *Agami karma* that he made during his life (before he died) and the *Sanchita* that is ready for transaction are still there. The part of the *Sanchita* that is ready will now determine the way and circumstances of his next birth and on and on the cycle continues. This is the endless cycle of birth and death that the scriptures refer to. What propels the person seeking *moksha*, is the burning desire to be free from this cycle of birth and death.

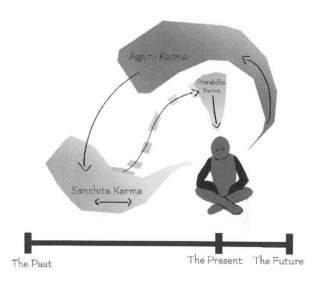

Figure 18. The 3 types of Karma

Now what happens to a person's *karma* load when he attains *Jivan Mukthi*? As we have seen *Jivan Mukthi* (Liberation while still alive) is attained when he has divorced himself from the sense of doer ship. So, he does no intentional actions. Where there is no action, no *karma* can be generated. Hence the day to day accruing of *Agami karma* stops. Throughout this lifetime, there will be no more *Agami karma* for him.

What happens to the *Sanchita karma*? First of all, it cannot grow since no *Agami* is being added to it. When a person attains *Jivan Mukthi*, all sense of doer ship is gone and when that happens, all the *karma* in his account, that had risen from his sense of doer ship, is gone. That means all the *Sanchita karma*, waiting to fructify in his account is gone. Everything accrued up to the moment of realizing the truth of *Tat tvam asi*, is gone.

The only *karma* left is the *Prarabdha karma*. This is the ripened *karma* (not the yet to fructify *karma*) of all his previous actions which he has started living out in this lifetime. Although, he is no longer a simple *jiva* but is a *Jivan Muktha*, the already matured karma load set aside for this lifetime still has to be lived out. As this plays out, because he is a *Jivan Muktha*, he does not get affected by them. He rides them out much like a drop of water on the lotus leaf. Just as the water does not wet or penetrate the leaf, the *Prarabdha karma* that is playing out, does not perturb the realized soul, the *jnani*.

Sanchita is gone, *Prarabdha* is exhausted and *Agami* is avoided and therefore there is no *Karma*. Since there is neither *punya* nor *paapa*, he does not acquire a new birth. As a result of knowledge (*Jnana*), he enjoys this *Jivan Mukti*. This is the fruit of knowledge (*Jnana Phalam*) and with this *Tattvabodha* completes its teaching.

This is the overview of how through knowledge, we can gain Liberation not only in this birth but also ultimately break free from future births.

- 12 -

CONCLUSION

I would like to close by presenting the hymn, *Nirvana Shatakam* also called *Atma Shatakam*. This was composed by *Adi Shankaracharya*, the presumed author of *Tattvabodha*, at the young age of 8. He had already mastered many spiritual teachings and was in search of his *guru* (teacher) to instruct him further. One day young *Shankara* met the learned *guru*, *Sri Govinda Bhagavatpada* and he wanted to become his disciple. The *guru* asked him, "Who are you?" The *guru* probably asked him this as a general question.

But to this question, *Shankara* is supposed to have composed the *Nirvana Shatakam* on the spot. After hearing it, the *guru* realized the depth of the young man and immediately accepted him as his disciple. This hymn summarizes the entire *Advaita Vedanta*. As you read this, visualize each line as an answer to the question, "Who are you?"

Nirvana Shatakam *(translated)*

I am not the mind, the intellect, the ego or the
memory,(*the internal instruments*)
I am not the ears, the skin, the nose or the
eyes,(*the sense organs*)
I am not space, not earth, not fire, water or
wind,(*the 5 elements*)
I am the form of consciousness and bliss,
I am the eternal Shiva*...

I am not the breath, nor the five vayus,
I am not the 7 tissues nor the 5 sheaths (*the 7
tissues in our body being plasma, blood, mus-
cle, fat, bone, nervous tissue/bone marrow and
sperm/ovum. We have seen the 5 sheaths*)
Nor am I the organs of speech, grasping, locomotion, elimination, procreation, (*this indicates
all the organs of action*)
I am the form of consciousness and bliss,
I am the eternal Shiva...

There is no like or dislike in me, no greed or
delusion,
I know not pride or jealousy,
I have no duty, no desire for wealth, lust

or liberation, (*the 4 human pursuits/ purusharthas*)
I am the form of consciousness and bliss,
I am the eternal Shiva ...

There is no virtue or vice for me, no pleasure or
    pain,
I need no mantras, no pilgrimage, no scriptures
    or rituals,
I am not the food, nor the eater of the food, nor
    the experience of eating
I am the form of consciousness and bliss,
I am the eternal Shiva ...

I have no fear of death, no caste or creed,
I have no father, no mother, for I was never born,
I am not a relative, nor a friend, nor a teacher nor
    a student,
I am the form of consciousness and bliss,
I am the eternal Shiva ...

I am devoid of duality, my form is formlessness,
I exist everywhere, pervading all senses,
I am neither attached, neither free nor captive,
I am the form of consciousness and bliss,
I am the eternal Shiva ...

Shiva here refers to one of the gods of the Hindu trinity of gods (*Brahma* the creator, *Vishnu* the protector and *Shiva* the destroyer) *Shiva* is known for being in deep meditation and is considered to be the ultimate *yogi*.

This was the depth of wisdom of young *Shankara*. All this knowledge he sang forth in response to the simple question, "Who are you?" That is how profound the question of identity is. The true "I" we seek is beyond anything we think of as "me". As discussed on (page 176), in the material world of our everyday life, we can use our regular CV. But to ourselves, when we are alone, in front of the mirror, when we seem besieged by trials and sorrow, we need to recall our true identity, that of the eternal, all pervading, limitless *Atma*. For example, to the world, I may be a doctor, Ayurvedic Practitioner and a teacher, a daughter to my parents, a wife to my husband and a mother to my son but to myself, I am eternal, all pervasive limitless *Brahman*.

Attaining this state is the aim of seekers on the path of spirituality.

This entire exercise is neither easy nor is it to be taken lightly. *Advaita Vedanta* cannot be grasped by reading one book or one hundred books. The role of a *guru* is a vital component in this undertaking. But in the current times where there are many false *gurus* contaminating the real *guru-shishya parampara* (teacher-student tradition), there is a natural hesitancy.

Should we give up or not start our studies at all, because we have not found the right teacher? No. We can start preparing for the study, by working on the 4 qualifications, by practicing *karma yoga* and *upasana yoga* by ourselves. This process itself may take us many years as the mind readies itself for *jnana yoga*. And when we are ready, the teacher will present himself. This is the fervent hope of all seekers.

I hope you have enjoyed coming on this journey with me.

Tat Tvam Asi

Acknowledgments

I would like to thank my husband, Sriram. His steady presence sustains me, and his unconditional love nourishes me in every step of my journey. I would like to express my gratitude to my son, Ashwath. His constant encouragement and untiring efforts towards ensuring perfection have pushed me to put thoughts into action and publish this effort. My salutations to my meditation teacher Ms. Alli Natesh, who introduced me to the path to Self-Knowledge. My heartfelt gratitude to my friend Ms. Susan Das who read and reread this book from its inception and infused confidence and hope at every stage.

I would also like to thank Ms. Hanna Bischof, a budding young illustrator, whose art adorns this book.

APPENDIX

Quick Reference

The 6 philosophies   14

1. *Nyaya*
2. *Vaisheshika*
3. *Sankya*
4. *Yoga*
5. *Mimansa*
6. *Vedanta*

◆ ◆ ◆

The 3 types of *Vedanta*   18

1. *Dvaita*
2. *Advaita*
3. *Vishistadvaita*

◆ ◆ ◆

The 4 human pursuits   22

1. *Dharma*: pursuit of the right way of life, ethics
2. *Artha*: pursuit of the basic essentials of life, like money, security
3. *Kama*: pursuit of luxury, sensual pleasures
4. *Moksha*: pursuit of Liberation

◆ ◆ ◆

The 4 stages of life   26

1. *Brahmacharya*: student stage
2. *Grihasta*: householder stage
3. *Vanaprastha*: preparing for renunciation/Self-Knowledge
4. *Sanyasa*: renunciate stage, time for Self-Knowledge

◆ ◆ ◆

The 4 qualifications   32

1. *Viveka*: discrimination
2. *Viraga*: dispassion
3. *Mumukshutvam*: desire for freedom

4. 6 fold discipline
    - *Shama*: tranquility of mind
    - *Dama*: control over the senses
    - *Uparama*: introspection
    - *Titiksha*: forbearance
    - *Shradha*: faith
    - *Samadanam*: concentration

The 3 types of *yogas*   51

1. *Karma yoga*: doing right action with right attitude
2. *Upasana yoga*: conditioning of the body and mind and senses
3. *Jnana yoga*: getting the right knowledge

The 8 limbs of *yoga*   62

1. *Yamas*: "Don't"s
    - Non Violence
    - Truthfulness
    - Non stealing

- Sexual restraint
- Non greed

2. *Niyamas*: "Do"s
   - Cleanliness
   - Contentment
   - Perseverance
   - Self study
   - Contemplation of *Brahman*

3. *Asanas*
4. *Pranayama*
5. *Pratyahara*
6. *Dharana*
7. *Dyana*
8. *Samadhi*

The 3 stages of study   80

1. *Shravanam*
2. *Mananam*
3. *Nidhidyasanam*

The 3 bodies   98

1. Gross body
2. Subtle body
3. Causal body

◆ ◆ ◆

The 19 parts of the subtle body   104

1. The 5 organs of knowledge
   - Ears/Sound
   - Touch/Skin
   - Eyes/Sight
   - Tongue/Taste
   - Nose/Smell
2. The 5 organs of action
   - Tongue/Speech
   - Hands/Grasping
   - Feet/Locomotion
   - Organ of excretion
   - Organ of procreation
3. The 4 internal instruments
   - Mind

- Memory
- Intellect
- Ego
4. The 5 *pranas*
  - *Prana*
  - *Udana*
  - *Vyana*
  - *Samana*
  - *Apana*

◆ ◆ ◆

1. Food/physical sheath
2. Vital Air/energy sheath
3. Mind/Psychological sheath
4. Intellectual sheath
5. Bliss sheath

◆ ◆ ◆

1. Waking state

1. *Agami*: *karma* from the actions that we do every day, which is being added to the master account; *Sanchita*
2. *Prarabdha*: actions that have fructified and are unfolding now
3. *Sanchita*: *karma* in master account awaiting fruition

Putting it all together: Relationship between the macrocosm and the microcosm

Principle	Macrocosm	Microcosm
Self	Brahman	Atma
Self (another name)	Paramatma	Jivatma
Causal	Causal matter	Karana Sharira
Subtle	Subtle matter	Sukshma Sharira
Gross	Gross matter	Sthula Sharira
Anatma (material principle)	Maya	Upadhis (5 sheaths, 3 bodies)
Self + Material principle	Brahman + Maya	Atma + Upadhis
Name given to Self + Material principle	Ishvara	Jiva
Sattva	Revealing power	Mode of Awareness. Knowledge
Rajas	Projecting power	Mode of Passion, doing, "I want…"
Tamas	Veiling power, Matter, insentient, inert	Mode of Inaction, cannot act, cannot learn, "I feel…"

SOURCES

1. *Tattvabodhaḥ*
   Saraswati - Arsha Vidya, Research and Publication Trust – 2012
2. http://explorevedanta.com/

ABOUT THE AUTHOR

Mithun Baliga is an Indian born medical doctor living in Atlanta, GA. After practicing medicine in India, United Kingdom and United States, she is now an Ayurvedic Health Counselor and Practitioner. Using Ayurveda, the ancient holistic health science of India she helps people improve their health through better diet and lifestyle. She also practices and teaches meditation. She integrates her knowledge of western medicine with Ayurveda and mind body soul medicine to help and guide people in their own personal journeys.

She loves to teach, travel, and volunteer. She lives with her husband and 15 year old son.

www.lotushouseofhealing.com

Made in the USA
Coppell, TX
25 May 2023

17302613R00155